Weston-super-Mare

The town and its seaside heritage

Weston-super-Mare

The town and its seaside heritage

Allan Brodie, Johanna Roethe and Kate Hudson-McAulay

Published by Historic England, The Engine House, Fire Fly Avenue, Swindon SN2 2EH
www.HistoricEngland.org.uk

Historic England is a Government service championing England's heritage and giving expert, constructive advice.

Images (except as otherwise shown with their captions) are © Historic England Archive; Fig 73 is © Crown Copyright. Historic England Archive; Fig 47 is Historic England Archive (RAF Photography); the images on p 26 and p 96 and Figs 18, 66, 72 and 82 are Historic England Archive (Aerofilms Collection); Fig 16 is an 1886 Ordnance Survey map using WebGIS, Grid Ref ST 31 61 © Crown Copyright (and database rights) 2019 and Landmark Information Group Ltd (All rights reserved 2019) Licence number 000394 and TP0024; and Map 1 and Map 2 on p 138 and p 142 are © Crown Copyright (and database rights) 2019. OS100024900

First published 2019

ISBN 978-1-84802-479-3

British Library Cataloguing in Publication data
A CIP catalogue record for this book is available from the British Library.

For more information about images from the Archive, contact Archives Services Team, Historic England, The Engine House, Fire Fly Avenue, Swindon SN2 2EH; telephone (01793) 414600.

Brought to publication by Victoria Trainor, Publishing, Historic England.

Typeset in Georgia Pro Light 9.25/13pt

Edited by Kathryn Glendenning
Page layout by Hybert Design
Proof read by Kim Bishop
Printed in Belgium by Graphius

Front cover
A view of Knightstone Island at high tide, with the sea washing over the causeway that links it to the mainland.
[DP218326]

Inside front cover
The former diving platform of the Open-Air Pool was photographed to mark its completion in 1937.
[BB81/08506]

Frontispiece
The Lodge on the left leads into Grove Park, while Grove Lane leads up the hill to housing, added from the 1860s onwards.
[DP218402]

Inside back cover
Birnbeck Pier emerging from sea mist.
[DP218547]

Contents

Acknowledgements

The authors would like to thank our colleagues in Historic England and North Somerset Council for their help and support. Members of the Heritage Action Zone (HAZ) committee have shared their expertise and we would like to thank them for their support. Particular mention should go to Cara MacMahon, the Heritage Action Zone Project Officer, who has been at the heart of coordinating the committee's work.

We have been fortunate to have valuable comments from Mark Bowden and Lucy Jessop, of Historic England. Edward Carpenter has carried out detailed research on the 20th-century archaeology of Weston-super-Mare from Historic England's aerial photography collection and this has provided us with valuable insights into the town's recent history. We have also been fortunate to spend time with Joanna Smith and Matthew Whitfield, who have shared their expertise on the development of the town's suburbs. This book benefits from the great expertise of our colleagues in the photographic and graphics teams. Steven Baker has taken several hundred photographs in support of the HAZ and we have been able to use many of these in this book. He has shown great perseverance in waiting for the right light, weather and tides to create the wonderful images that can be found throughout the book.

We would also like to thank James Davies for his support and advice regarding our illustrations. Damian Grady has flown over Weston-super-Mare twice and created a wonderful modern resource that complements our historic collections, and Amy Wright has produced the very accomplished maps for the gazetteer.

We are also grateful to Councillor John Crockford-Hawley, who had the patience to pick through all our research material and greatly improve it. Andrew Mason, of the Birnbeck Pier Trust, and his colleagues have kindly taken the time to share their knowledge of the pier and we were fortunate to be able to visit the island with them. Delia Gaze, whose family once owned the Royal Pier Hotel, shared her memories and images of Weston-super-Mare in the 1960s. She still regrets cutting up the football that the Beatles signed for her to sell the pieces to her school friends!

Sarah Bowen, of the North Somerset Library Service, allowed us to make use of its extensive collection of images to illustrate this book. We have also enjoyed using the Local Studies collection at Weston-super-Mare Library, with its unrivalled collection of material about the town's history, and the extensive collection of building control plans at Somerset Archives, Taunton. The staff at Weston Museum have also been very helpful and informative, including allowing us to photograph the 1961 model of the proposed town centre development. Amal Khreisheh, Curator of Archaeology at Somerset Museums Service, helped us to obtain key images to explain the town's development.

We would like to thank the people of Weston-super-Mare for their interest and support, and not forgetting all those people who have visited Weston over the years and added so much to its colourful story. In particular we would like to remember Johanna's late friend Regine Gerhardt, who had happy memories of her visit to Weston.

Foreword

Weston-super-Mare is on the cusp of an exciting new chapter in its history.

It possesses an extraordinarily rich architectural heritage that stems from its enduring appeal as a popular and prominent seaside resort. The legacy of historic street patterns, Victorian terraces, parks and piers, as well as many other exquisite architectural features, provides the town with a tremendous foundation on which to build its future and achieve a prosperous year-round economy.

North Somerset Council recognises the potential of the town's historic past. It is actively promoting projects that take inspiration from heritage to boost the quality and diversity of local businesses and housing. At the same time, new partnerships are being established with public sector and local stakeholders to raise awareness of the heritage value and the cultural potential of the town.

One of these partnerships is a Heritage Action Zone between the Council and Historic England. This involves a range of projects designed to understand better the qualities that make Weston attractive and unique. The programme addresses issues to help reinforce and enhance that character, whilst sensitively managing new investment and pressures for change. Research has been carefully undertaken to study how Weston originated, how it developed and to establish the significance of what survives today. Sharing this new knowledge with the town's residential, business and visitor communities, as well as potential investors, is helping to raise awareness of how heritage can be the vital factor that helps Weston to grow and flourish.

This book is one of the first tangible products of the Heritage Action Zone. It is designed to spread Weston's appeal to the widest possible audience and celebrates the town's colourful history and heritage. We commend it to all on that basis and in the certainty that Weston will be revealed in a fascinating new light.

Sir Laurie Magnus
Chairman, Historic England

Cllr Nigel Ashton
Leader of North Somerset Council

1

Introduction

In March 2017 Weston-super-Mare was chosen as one of the 10 successful bids for support from Historic England through the creation of Heritage Action Zones (HAZ). Historic England will invest £6 million to help bring these 10 historic places back to life and to stimulate economic growth. A further eight zones were announced in December 2017, and more applications have been invited for 2019/20. Funding can provide Repair Grants for listed buildings, scheduled monuments and registered parks and gardens, and Capacity Building Grants for wider area-based schemes. Historic England is also using its expertise to stimulate regeneration in the designated areas. Support may include providing research into historic sites or buildings, and offering advice and training about repairs and finding new uses for buildings. It may also involve making improvements to entries on the National Heritage List for England (NHLE) to clarify where change may be possible. To be selected, a proposed Heritage Action Zone needs the support of public, private and third-sector organisations and at least one local authority. It is also necessary to demonstrate that there are opportunities for sustainable long-term growth in these historic places through making better use of local heritage assets.

It is perhaps significant that in the first group of ten successful bids, two were seaside resorts: Weston-super-Mare and Ramsgate. The lure of foreign sunshine, changes in lifestyle and a growth in the number of short breaks and day trips have all contributed to a decline in the number of people taking their long summer holiday at the English seaside. Since World War II, there has been consistent underinvestment in seaside resorts and a consequent decline in the state of repair of buildings and attractions. Many seaside houses have suffered from unsympathetic subdivision, with property owners seeking to maximise the return on their investment by creating houses in multiple occupation (HMO). Also, as the ground floor is the economically active part of many seafront and town centre buildings, it may receive investment to make a business eye-catching, while the rest of the structure is frequently left neglected.

Seaside resorts have also suffered from long-term economic problems arising in part from the seasonal and casual nature of their leading industry. Additionally, many resorts have large numbers of economically inactive residents, high numbers of people with low skills and higher-than-average crime rates. Therefore, it is common to find seaside resorts figuring prominently among the most deprived places in the government's Indices

This is a slice of Weston-super-Mare's architecture, seen from the end of the Grand Pier. In the foreground is Knightstone Island, with Holy Trinity Church at the top of the hillside, beneath Worlebury Hill Fort. [DP218765]

of Multiple Deprivation. To add to the problems of seaside resorts, anthropogenic climate change is leading to a rise in sea level and increased storminess, necessitating the costly and potentially visually intrusive reconfiguration of many seafronts.

While there may be no magic wand to solve the social and economic problems of seaside resorts, many of these towns have recognised that they are attractive locations, with a strong local community and an interesting heritage that can contribute to economic revival and physical renewal. North Somerset Council has acknowledged that making Weston-super-Mare a better place in which to live, study and work will also make it a better place to visit. The subtitle of the master plan for the future of the town is 'Living, Learning, Lifestyles', and a significant strand in this document is to make the most of Weston's historic environment.[1]

Historic England's decision to create a Heritage Action Zone in Weston-super-Mare is supporting the local authority's programme in a number of ways. It is making money available for grants to improve historic buildings within conservation areas. The environmental consultancy LUC has also been commissioned to carry out a study to assess and map patterns of historic character across Weston-super-Mare and its adjacent seascape.[2] The architecture and urban planning practice Allies & Morrison has conducted a review of Weston's conservation areas and their boundaries, prior to the development of conservation area management plans.[3]

Historic England is also using its own resources to provide advice and support. A number of listed building entries have been updated and made more precise, and new structures, including the town's railway station, have been added to the NHLE. Members of Historic England's Historic Places Investigation Team in Swindon have carried out detailed research and fieldwork, and have compiled extensive research materials and a gazetteer for use by Historic England, North Somerset Council and the people of Weston-super-Mare. A study of the archaeology of the town as captured in aerial photographs has been carried out by the Aerial Investigation and Mapping Team in Swindon. New terrestrial and aerial photography has also been undertaken to assist the research programme, and to provide illustrations and exhibition material to promote the work of the HAZ.

This book is also a product of Historic England's research programme. It tells the story of Weston-super-Mare as a historic town and a popular destination for holidaymakers for 200 years. It also outlines in greater detail the challenges facing Weston today and how the town's rich heritage can contribute to its future success.

Weston-super-Mare before the railway

Weston-super-Mare first developed on land at the base of Worlebury Hill, a short distance inland from the sea (Fig 1). The hill was used for grazing animals, at least until the early 19th century, and early maps suggest that four large fields were arranged along its lower slopes. To the south was a large expanse of marshy land and moorland, separated from the sea by 'sand tots', the local dialect term for sandhills.

Located on the Severn Estuary, Weston-super-Mare enjoys, or perhaps endures, the second-highest tidal range in the world, meaning that because of its shallow, sandy beach, the sea can appear very distant at low tide. A 1913 guidebook noted, 'The Sands are to many Weston's chief attraction.' However, it then went on to record, 'Beyond the sand is a considerable expanse of exceptionally sticky mud.'[4]

Domesday Book records the manors of Ashcombe, Uphill, Worle, Kewstoke and Milton. Worle boasts a small Norman motte-and-bailey castle known as Castle Batch, and a church with 12th-century origins, while the church of St Nicholas at Uphill is of a similar age. The name Weston, and specific names such as Worthy and the 'hay' in Blakehay, may imply a settlement with Saxon origins. However, Weston's parish church, St John the Baptist, at the foot of Worlebury Hill, is first mentioned only in 1226, though it seems to have been constructed some time before this.

The medieval parish church was demolished in 1824 and replaced by a new church (*see* p 22), but it is known from engravings, fragments in Weston Museum and contemporary descriptions. These include the testimonies of old inhabitants of Weston gathered by the solicitor, local historian and author Ernest Baker during the early 1880s. In 1791 the clergyman and historian the Revd John Collinson (1757–93) briefly described the form of the church: 'The church, which is dedicated to St. John the Baptist, is a small building of one pace [piece], 84 feet in length and 20 in breadth, having at the west end a tower in which hang three bells.'[5] The testimonies gathered by Baker suggest a church with Norman origins, which was largely remodelled and reconstructed during the 15th century. Fragments in Weston Museum and the presence of a Norman font bowl provide evidence of its early origins, though fonts can easily be moved around. Engravings suggest that the parish church had a tower and an

This modern aerial photograph, taken from the north, shows Knightstone Island, the Grand Pier and the length of the beach. In the distance can be seen Uphill, to the south of Weston, and Brean Down, in the top right of the photograph.
[NMR 33066/099]

5

aisleless nave with a southern porch and an aisleless choir with a door in the south wall. The tracery looks as if it may be a 15th-century Perpendicular design, while the tower seems to have earlier tracery, possibly Y-tracery dating from the 14th century. The door in the north wall of the nave and the two lancets are of early Gothic character, implying a date of around 1200 for the body of the nave (Fig 2).

Standing a short height above sea level (between the 10m and 15m contour lines), the church survived the worst natural disaster to befall the Severn Estuary. On 30 January 1607 a devastating flood took place in the estuary due to what may have been a form of tsunami, resulting in around 2,000 deaths by

Figure 1
This modern aerial photograph, taken from the south, shows the wooded Worlebury Hill to the north of the town, with housing on its slopes. Also prominent is the wide, flat beach and the land behind it, where most of the town has been built.
[NMR 33066/023]

drowning. Floodwaters may have been as deep as 3.7m and any low-lying properties at Weston-super-Mare would have been badly damaged or destroyed.

Despite the settlement's demonstrated vulnerability to flooding, it continued to be inhabited – a survey of church lands by Parliament returned in 1653 stated that 'the parish of Weston-super-Mare consisted of about five and 30 famelys'.[6] These families made their living by fishing, farming, teasel growing and collecting seaweed for fertiliser, and later by providing potash for glassworks in Bristol. In the 17th century there was a windmill on the hilltop and numerous pits in the hill. (Calamine, an ore of zinc, was mined from these pits for use in brass founding from the 1560s onwards.) At the end of the 17th century there are references to works being carried out on sea defences, but these would probably have been inadequate to deal with a huge storm on 26 November 1703, described vividly by Daniel Defoe (1660–1731) in *The Storm*, which was published a year later.[7]

Weston's first visitors

In 1696 the manor of Weston-super-Mare came into the hands of the Pigott family and during the 18th century they may have constructed a small cottage for their use, which was enlarged during the 1770s and 1780s into the more substantial Grove House. The Glebe House, the rectory beside the parish church, was similarly improved during the late 18th and early 19th century. By 1790 the Revd Wadham Pigott was the curate in charge of the parish and during his brother's prolonged absences he became the de facto squire.

The Revd Wadham Pigott was the first high-status resident of Weston-super-Mare, but visitors of note had been coming, at least occasionally, to the settlement since the late 17th century to study its interesting natural character. By the 1770s the area around Weston-super-Mare was already being recognised for its health-giving qualities. The writer, social reformer and philanthropist Hannah More (1745–1833) went to Uphill in 1773 to convalesce. Her presence led Dr Langhorne, rector of the Somerset village of Blagdon since 1766, to visit Weston. Another local clergyman and friend of Hannah More, the Revd William Leeves (1748–1828), rector of Wrington, found Weston to be sufficiently alluring that he built himself a cottage overlooking the sea in about 1791 (Fig 3).

Figure 2
This illustration of the medieval parish church accompanied a description of the church and early Weston-super-Mare written by a local solicitor, George Bennett, in the Gentleman's Magazine *in 1805. It also includes a view of the Revd William Leeves's cottage, probably the only other building in Weston considered worthy of illustration (see also Fig 3).*
[Reproduced by kind permission of Somerset Archaeological and Natural History Society. SHC A\DAS\1\439\1(2A)]

Figure 3
William Leeves's cottage still survives in a recognisable
form today as The Old Thatched Cottage Restaurant on
Knightstone Road.
[DP218417]

The earliest illustration of this building appears in the *Gentleman's Magazine* of 1805 (*see* Fig 2) and an 1847 guidebook described it as 'a quaint and curious structure with a high thatched roof and square-headed windows'.[8]

In April 1797 an advertisement in *Bonner & Middleton's Bristol Journal* sought to entice sea bathers to Uphill in search of a healthy summer location, but despite such advertisements no development relating to sea bathing at Uphill followed. Instead, Weston-super-Mare became the focus of attention during the 19th century. In 1805 the same *Gentleman's Magazine* article that illustrated Leeves's cottage and the medieval parish church provided a brief description of the village:

> This village is much frequented of late in Summer and Autumn for the benefit of sea air and bathing; several good lodging-houses having been lately erected for the reception of company. And the Rev. Mr Leeves of Wrington has built a charming little cottage on the beach, at which himself and [his] family reside a considerable part of the year.[9]

As well as writers and clergymen, Weston-super-Mare was also beginning to catch the eye of artists; George Cumberland (1754–1848), a writer on art and a watercolour painter, moved to Weston in 1803, before settling in Bristol in 1807. The village's proximity to Bristol and Bath undoubtedly explains a small but growing interest in Weston's aesthetic, as well as curative, properties, despite its challenging road connections for coach travellers. In 1822 it still took five hours to travel between Bath and Weston-super-Mare.

The fledgling resort

In the 1880s, elderly resident Samuel Norvill recalled Weston as it was in the early 19th century, a small village without a hotel, public house or shop:

> There was no High Street: it was called The Street, and very narrow it was too, there was only just room for one putt or cart to pass down it at a time. On the East side there was a ditch, and on the West a hedge banked up with stones to keep the earth back. The street itself was always very muddy and dirty; some stones were thrown down loosely on one side to make a sort of footpath … Midway there was a withy bed, in which refuse fish were generally thrown … Nearly everybody kept geese, they paid so well; you see, they could run about over the common all day, and so didn't cost much to keep.[10]

'The Street', which would later become the High Street, ran from north to south. From its northern end, heading eastwards, was the road to Bristol. At the south end of The Street was Watersill Road, the precursor of modern Regent Street. From this point another lane wandered into the meadow and orchard, where today's Meadow and Orchard Streets were later established. There was a cluster of houses on either side of the southern end of The Street and a few between The Street and the sea, as well as a handful further inland. At the beginning of the 19th century, there were also three cottages on the hillside above the village, up what would now be Grove Lane, including one occupied by Richard Muggleworth and another that was used as a lodging house.

The main figures behind the first stages of Weston's development were Richard Parsley (1767–1846) and William Cox. It has been suggested that Parsley came from Yorkshire, but on his marriage certificate to Elizabeth 'Betty' Wakeley, on 8 January 1793, he described himself as being from Kewstoke (3 miles north of Weston), at least by that date (Fig 4). He farmed Worlebury Hill with a flock of 1,000 sheep until it was planted with trees during the early 1820s. He was also Overseer of the Poor and churchwarden during the 1790s and later steward of the manor. Therefore, he would have been well known to the Pigott family, the lords of the manor, and it may have been through them that he came to know William Cox, from Brockley, in Somerset. Their business partnership lasted until 1834, by which time Weston was emerging as a small town.

In the earliest stages of seaside resort development, the only requirements were access to the sea and a place to stay. In Georgian seaside resorts, any house, indeed any building, might provide lodgings for visitors, but there was a need for some better-quality accommodation, as well as some rooms that people might use on their first arrival, before finding longer-term lodgings. In seaside resorts that developed from pre-existing settlements, the village inn often served this purpose, but Weston-super-Mare had no such pre-existing facility. Therefore the town's first hotel was built between 1807 or 1808 and 1810, on the seafront south of Knightstone Island. This project was undertaken by Parsley and Cox in partnership with James Partridge Capell, the tenant of the farm at Ashcombe, and Richard Fry. In 1810 the hotel was leased to James Needham, a Bristol hotelier, and it opened in July of that year.

This financial gamble does not seem to have paid off immediately for its investors, as the doors of the hotel closed through a lack of custom in 1811 and it was put up for sale by auction. The building remained closed for three years, but by 1814 a sufficient number of visitors seem to have arrived to merit its reopening. Originally known simply as The Hotel, it is subsequently referred to in guidebooks as Fry's Hotel, Reeve's or Reeves' Hotel, then by the 1850s 'Reeve's Hotel, conducted by Mr Thomas Rogers' and by 1855 'Royal [late Reeve's] Hotel conducted by Mr T Rogers'.[11] A map of 1853 shows the main body of the Royal Hotel as it stands today, the extension to the original structure seeming to date from 1849 (Fig 5).

At the time that the early part of the hotel was being constructed, Parsley and Cox were acquiring land on which to construct new housing, with a view to

Figure 4
This gravestone, in the churchyard of St John the Baptist parish church, commemorates the life of Richard Parsley, who died in 1846 aged 79. It also remembers the life of his wife and other members of his family. [DP218497]

Figure 5
Early maps show the Royal Hotel to have been a much smaller building, which matches the southern three bays of the current hotel (on the right-hand side in this photograph). The end of the original building appears to have been where the almost-central block breaks forward. [DP218422]

turning the village into a popular destination for visitors. The Pigott Estate sold them land and they began acquiring the common rights attached to the 'Auster Tenements', small cottages or hovels with historic rights of common.[12] An Enclosure Act was sought to establish the basic infrastructure for the settlement by concentrating land ownership in the hands of the small number of men who would drive development. Inevitably, the key beneficiaries would be Parsley and Cox, who would acquire most land.

The Weston-super-Mare Enclosure Act 1810 covered 993 acres of land and James Staples was appointed as Commissioner in June 1810, with responsibility for 'setting out, allotting, dividing and inclosing the said moors, commons and waste lands and common fields and otherwise putting the Act into execution'.[13] He oversaw the creation of new roads, tracks and hedges and the digging of ditches, building walls and stabilising sand dunes. The Commissioner specified that the Town Quarry and the Manor Road Quarry could be used for the repair of roads within the parish of Weston-super-Mare (*see* Fig 57). To fund the development programme, three auctions were held between July 1811 and February 1812. The average selling price of 1,381s per acre made this the most expensive enclosure land in North Somerset in its day, and was a reflection of the potential value of landholding and owning property in an emerging seaside resort. The cost of maintaining and repairing roads, footpaths, bridges, etc was to be met by the main beneficiaries of the Act, including Cox and Parsley, James P Capell at Ashcombe, John Pigott and his brother the Revd Wadham Pigott.

By the time the enclosure process had been completed in 1815, an outline for the shape of the future development of Weston-super-Mare had been established. The sales of parcels of seafront land paved the way for the development of Richmond Street, Oxford Street and Carlton Street, while some of Weston's first seafront villas began to be built. At the time of the Enclosure, the seafront to the south of Watersill Road, the future Regent Street, was largely sand dunes. Behind these dunes were sandy fields in which Parsley farmed teasels, an important product in the manufacturing of cloth.

New, larger and more expensive houses began to appear. For instance, Isaac Jacobs, a Bristol glass merchant, built Belvedere in 1811 facing Beach Road. The 1822 guidebook stated, 'A handsome pile of building, never yet occupied, erected by Mr Jacobs of Bristol, terminates this part of the village, which is frequently styled Jacobs Town.'[14] Money difficulties forced Jacobs to sell Belvedere in 1819 and by 1847 it had been subdivided, with one half being used as an academy for young gentlemen preparing for university. It was demolished in 1925. Richard Parsley erected his substantial, at least by early Weston standards, Georgian house, not on the seafront but from where he could oversee his newly created Whitecross Estate (behind the future site of the

Figure 6
Richard Parsley's Whitecross House was originally
three bays wide and symmetrical. A fourth bay in a
similar style was added on the eastern side between
1903 and 1931, by which time the building was being
used as a Sunday school.
[DP218260]

Victoria Methodist Church, on what was to become Station Road). It appears on the 1838 tithe map and was described in an 1840 guidebook as 'newly-erected'.[15] The house is now part of a community facility associated with the church, which hides it from public view (Fig 6).

While some houses were being built on previously undeveloped land, the replacement of pre-existing houses was already under way. An elderly resident recorded by Ernest Baker during the early 1880s recalls walking along the side of the stream to three cottages, which were demolished to make way for the first Waterloo House, built in 1816.

By this date numerous houses were being built, rebuilt or refurbished to provide lodgings for visitors. The 1811 Census recorded that Weston's population of 125 lived in 30 inhabited buildings; by 1821 its 738 inhabitants occupied 126 buildings, while a decade later, the population of 1,310 lived in 218 houses. Rutter's guidebook of 1829 claimed there were upwards of 150 lodging houses.[16] A more accurate statement might be that there were more than 150 houses where rooms were being let to lodgers, the standard practice in Georgian seaside resorts to meet the accommodation needs of visitors.

Small hotels also began to be built. In 1819 Weston's second hotel, the Mason's Arms (later known as the Bath Hotel and the Imperial), opened on the new South Parade. The Plough Hotel opened on the High Street in 1819, becoming Weston's third hotel. An advertisement in the *Bristol Mirror* in May 1819, placed by the proprietor Christopher Kingdon, noted that 'the Larder will be liberally supplied, and the Wines may be relied upon as of the first Vintage'. The advert goes on to say, 'To the Beds much attention has been paid, and every care will be taken to keep them and the chambers well aired.'[17]

The growth of Weston-super-Mare relied on improved transport services and roads. A limited coach service between Bristol and Weston began in 1814, and soon a regular service was in place. On 26 April 1817 an advertisement for The Hotel in the *Bristol Mirror* stated that prospective visitors could use 'a Four-Horse COACH from the Hope and Anchor Redcliffe-Hill, every Wednesday and Saturday, at 2 o'clock'.[18] On 8 May 1819 John Harse and William Hill advertised that their coach, the Prince Regent, was to resume its regular, four-times-a-week service between Bristol and Weston-super-Mare in seven days' time. To attract customers, the advertisement said they had 'purchased an entirely new, elegant, safe, and commodious POST COACH' and had 'likewise engaged a steady, sober and experienced Coach-man'.[19] In 1806 Messrs Stabbins and Hill began a carrier service in the summer using wagons to bring goods and less affluent visitors, but this was short-lived. In 1811 John Harse revived the service with greater success. Two other carriers began operating in 1813 and by 1820 there were eight. Tourists were also beginning to arrive at Weston by sea; in June 1825 the first pleasure steamer called at the Knightstone Wharf, bringing in passengers from Newport in south Wales.

Sea bathing in the early 19th century

At the beginning of the 19th century, people came to Weston-super-Mare primarily for its health-giving properties. A newspaper advertisement in February 1811 for the sale of a house promoted the village by saying, 'Weston holds a distinguished claim to fashionable resort, and from the purity of its air, the most cheering hope is presented to the general Invalid, elasticity to the enervated, and to the convalescent the most abundant supplies.'[20] Weston's first guidebook in 1822 stated, 'The air is soft but bracing, and is particularly efficacious to those constitutions with which the Devonshire coast disagrees.'[21]

Access to the sea was problematic due to the distance that it retreated at low tide, and while bathing machines led the charge into the sea at most resorts, additional arrangements had to be made at Weston-super-Mare. The 1822 guidebook refers to three bathing machines on the sands, the time of their use being regulated by the tide, rather than by medical advice that stipulated that sea bathing was most effective first thing in the morning. However, at all times of the day there was bathing at Anchor Head, which was reserved for ladies. Betty Muggleworth managed the open sea bathing there, spreading an old sail between rocks to shelter ladies dressing and undressing.

Another means of overcoming the limitations on bathing caused by Weston's geography was to provide a bathhouse. A hot, saltwater bath had been opened in Somerset Place in the centre of the village, attended by Mrs Jane Gill, one of the original bathing women who accompanied female bathers into the sea. The water was hauled from the sea in a barrel, then stored in a tank over a boiler, in which it was heated. Mrs Gill's establishment also had a shower bath – a 'Punch and Judy box' arrangement in which the victim stood with curtains drawn around them while a bucket of seawater was poured over his or her head by an assistant standing on steps.[22]

From the 1820s onwards, Knightstone Island became the main centre for bathing. Prior to this it was used for fishing and was home to Weston's first coal yard. Therefore, it must have seemed a singularly unappealing, and unhealthy, part of the settlement during the early 19th century. Nevertheless, the first bathhouse and pool on Knightstone Island were constructed by Mr Howe of Bristol in 1820. Weston's first guidebook in 1822 recorded that 'three years ago Knightstone was a useless rock' but that 'a reading room, hot and cold baths and a lodging house have been erected on the island'.[23] Knightstone was still an island, connected to the mainland only by a ridge of pebbles, but when Thomas Pruen took it over, one of his main projects was the construction of a causeway. In 1829 a guidebook recorded that 'on this rock are three turreted houses, now let exclusively for lodgings. Its largest contains several handsome sitting apartments, with numerous bed-rooms, separate kitchens, coach house, and stables.'[24] The same guidebook also described the bathing facilities:

> On Knightstone are several hot and cold baths, plunging and shower baths of sea water, which were constructed at a considerable expence, and fitted up in a commodious manner, with every convenience; each bath having a private dressing-room attached to it, and every attention paid to the accommodation of the bathers. An open cold bath with dressing-rooms attached, has also been formed by enclosing a flat shelving portion of the rock, with a breakwater, within which the sea flows at high tide.[25]

On 5 August 1828 Knightstone Island was put up for auction and was acquired by Dr Edward Long Fox (1761–1835), a Quaker physician from Brislington House lunatic asylum in Bristol, who advocated sea bathing for the treatment of mental illness, as well as for physical complaints. He was assisted in his development of the island by his son, Dr Francis Ker Fox (1805–83). The bathhouse on Knightstone Island was built in 1832 and, despite damage in a fire in 1844, is now in use as offices and a salon (Fig 7).

The island was again up for sale in 1847, when it was described as 'one of the most complete Bathing Establishments in England'.[26] The bathhouse

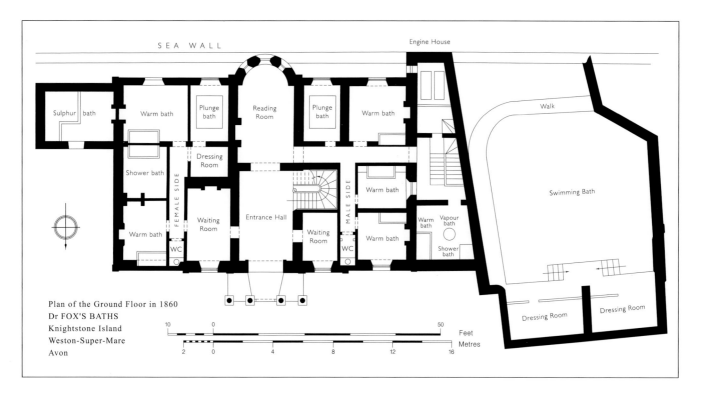

SEA WALL

Engine House

Sulphur bath

Warm bath

Plunge bath

Reading Room

Plunge bath

Warm bath

Walk

Shower bath

Dressing Room

FEMALE SIDE

Warm bath

Swimming Bath

Warm bath

Waiting Room

Entrance Hall

MALE SIDE

Warm bath

Warm bath

Vapour bath

Waiting Room

WC

Shower bath

WC

Plan of the Ground Floor in 1860
Dr FOX'S BATHS
Knightstone Island
Weston-Super-Mare
Avon

10   0   50
                                              Feet
                                              Metres
2   0   4   8   12   16

Dressing Room

Dressing Room

Figure 7 (left)
The Georgian bathhouse on Knightstone Island is five bays wide, with the central three bays breaking slightly forward and topped with a low, triangular pediment. The central door is covered by a rectangular porch.
[DP218642]

Figure 8 (above)
This plan of the bathhouse on Knightstone Island, as it was arranged in 1860, reveals that men (on the right) were separated from women by the central entrance hall.
[DMP/DFB001]

consisted on the ground floor of an entrance hall, a reading room and eight bath rooms with anterooms and water closets (Fig 8). On the first floor, there were three sitting rooms, seven bedrooms and a water closet, while the basement housed a kitchen, scullery and other offices, including a servants' hall and the boiler for hot water, steam apparatus, etc. Attached to the bathhouse were vapour and shower baths, and a large open swimming bath, well supplied with seawater, with three dressing rooms. There was also a sulphur bath, a dressing room and large cisterns for rain and seawater. Accompanying the bathhouse was a small house containing two sitting rooms and four bedrooms, with an underground kitchen and offices. There was also a row of three houses running from south-east to north-west, roughly on the site of the later swimming baths.

Weston in the 1820s

The 1822 guidebook recalled that not many years ago, Weston consisted of only 'a few huts' and the inhabitants had made their living by fishing. However, 'the purity of its air, added to its vicinity to Bath and Bristol, attracted the attention of valetudinarians; and the cures continually affected by the uncommon salubrity of its invigorating breezes, soon raised it to the station it now occupies amongst fashionable watering places'.[27] A measure of exaggeration due to local pride and a desire to attract customers is inevitable, but it is fitting that a site associated with health features prominently at the start of the guidebook. The frontispiece of the 1822 guidebook shows Knightstone Island, with just the main bathhouse building and some smaller structures around it. Despite proclaiming that Weston-super-Mare now occupies a station among fashionable watering places, the 1822 guidebook describes a small, not especially attractive village, with the first elements to cater for tourists beginning to be put in place. Having built up the village on page 5, the following page more than somewhat redresses the balance:

> Weston-super-Mare does not present a very inviting appearance to the stranger. The houses, scattered mostly without arrangement, and roofed with red tile, give a character of meanness to the village; and if a stranger first enters it on a stormy day and at low water, he may perhaps feel inclined to turn his horses and head towards home again.[28]

Weston's hotels were mentioned, as well as a number of the newest and larger houses that provided lodgings. The village already boasted a schoolroom of 1822 for 100 children, with a house for the master and mistress. The first small-scale private educational establishments had already begun to appear, and these would become an important feature of Weston later in the 19th century. Mr May ran a seminary for young gentlemen on the North Parade and Mrs Downman had an establishment for the education of young ladies in Wellington Place.

The 1822 guidebook also pointed people to the bathing facilities at Anchor Head and Knightstone, as well as to Mrs Gill's establishment in Somerset Place. However, there seems to have been little to entertain people for the rest of the day. There was a billiard table near the hotel and a reading room offering a fine view of the sea. There were two pleasure boats, *Princess Charlotte* and *Princess Mary*, which were kept for hire and run by experienced fishermen. People with an interest in nature might visit Brean Down, while others with an interest in killing nature could shoot on an expedition to Flat Holm and Steep Holm. A house had been erected on Flat Holm for the refreshment of visitors, who could admire the recently reglazed lighthouse. Jaunting cars, wheel chairs and sedan chairs, ponies and donkeys could be hired in the village to help visitors get around and enjoy excursions into the countryside and southwards to Uphill.

To safeguard the growing investment in the settlement, improved sea defences were required. The sand dunes would have afforded some protection to any properties lying behind them, but some attempts to consolidate them took place during the early 19th century. In 1814 the Revd Lewis, who lived at the beach end of Regent Street, requested that the sandbank nearest to his house should be covered with clay to prevent sand shifting into his street and 20 guineas was set aside to improve the bank. There was a high pebble beach from Knightstone to the Revd William Leeves's cottage and inside that was an artificial mudbank acting as a sea wall, with a walk along the top of it. This seems to have been established in 1826 and is presumably related to the greater use being made of Knightstone Island. This bank was extended to where Regent Street was located in 1829. A new esplanade was created on the site of the former sand dunes that had been levelled during enclosure. It was a gravelled path fronted by a low wall and is depicted in an oil painting of around 1860 by William Henry Hopkins (1825–92) (Fig 9).

By the time John Rutter's guidebook was published in 1829, modest but significant additions had been made to the village's building stock. The parish church had been rebuilt and the first places of worship for Nonconformists had been established. Rutter's guidebook reported, 'In fashionable and public amusements, Weston must be acknowledged to be deficient; "health, not dissipation" is the lure it presents.'[29] Nevertheless, Rutter described the assembly rooms that were erected in 1826 by John Thorn, which consisted of 'a handsome suite of rooms on the first floor, the largest is 40 feet by 20, and commands a fine view of the bay. On the ground floor are other large and commodious apartments.'[30] Assembly rooms, even modest ones like this

example, provided Georgian tourists with a venue for taking tea, playing cards and dancing during the afternoons and evenings. By 1840 the assembly rooms had been taken over by Joseph Whereat (1813–65), a printer, publisher and engraver, who created a library on the ground floor (Fig 10).

Another essential of the Georgian entertainment scene was the circulating library, a venue for socialising, borrowing books, buying holiday essentials and gathering information about visitors and accommodation. The 1822 guide mentioned briefly a reading room, but seven years later Rutter provided a little

Figure 9
This oil painting by William Henry Hopkins dates from around 1860. It shows the nature of the beach, sea wall and esplanade at Weston-super-Mare at that time. Painted at low water, the extensive sandy shore is visible.
[Reproduced by kind permission of North Somerset Council and South West Heritage Trust, 2019. WESTM: 326]

Figure 10
An illustration of Joseph Whereat's library and assembly rooms appears in an 1847 guidebook (Anon 1847). Remarkably for a modest building in a very prominent location, this structure has survived and has been incorporated into the complex of buildings facing the Grand Pier. This complex also includes the former Beach Hotel at the end of Regent Street.
[North Somerset Library Service]

more information: 'On the North Parade is a good library and the convenient reading room. It is kept by Mr Richard Hill, who has a book in which all visitors, on their arrival, should cause the names and local address to be inserted; and where may be inspected a list of the unoccupied lodgings.'[31] By 1840 Hill's facility was being rivalled by Whereat's, created in the assembly rooms building. In 1827 Weston acquired its first market house, built by Richard Parsley behind the High Street, where the Playhouse now stands.

The parish church, St John the Baptist, was reconstructed in 1824–5, between the publication of Weston's first two guidebooks in 1822 and 1829. The *Gentleman's Magazine* in 1805 had described the poor state of repair of the building:

> I was sorry to see the roof and windows of this room [the vestry-room] in so bad a state of repair; the tiling being gone from some parts, exposed this venerable little Consistory to the inclemency of the weather. The roof and windows of the Church and Chancel also are in a sad state of repair; one window in particular on the North side of the Chancel I observed to be much broken, and where the glass is wanting, its place supplied by bundles of hay.[32]

The medieval church was in a poor state of repair, but was also too small for the rapidly growing village and its increasing number of visitors. The reconstruction fund was kick-started by a donation of £1,000 by the Revd Wadham Pigott. The old church was pulled down in 1824 and its replacement had opened by the following year. The new structure could accommodate a congregation of 1,000 and had sufficient space for visitors as well as residents (Fig 11). By the time his guidebook was published in 1829, Rutter could claim that the church was 'a neat modern structure'. He went on to describe it as it existed before the extensive later additions and alterations: 'It is large and commodious, consisting of a nave, 60 feet by 40, with a square tower, a chancel, and a projecting chapel on its northern side.'[33]

The interior was lavish, at least in comparison with its predecessor:

The chancel has two windows and a centre doorway to the south. It is supported by three well-wrought buttresses, and attached to the south east angle of the new church, into which it opens by a large pointed arch. The ceiling of the chancel is ribbed, with ornamented bosses at the intersections alternately with a few shields, one charged with three clarions, and another with three roses.[34]

Weston on the eve of the railway age

For Weston-super-Mare, the 1830s was a decade of consolidation and steady growth, building on its reputation as a pleasant, healthy place to visit and to live in. As has been mentioned, the most significant event of the decade was the reconstruction and improvement of Dr Fox's bathhouse on Knightstone Island. By the end of the decade, much of the settlement's new development was beginning to be orientated towards the bathhouse, rather than southwards along the beach, as had occurred previously.

The 1831 Census recorded that the population of Weston was 1,310 and there were 218 inhabited houses, with a further 8 being constructed and 52 uninhabited, a surprisingly large number. As the Census was enumerated on 30 May, there may have been some visitors present, but at least some of the 52 unoccupied houses may have been properties in use as lodgings only during the

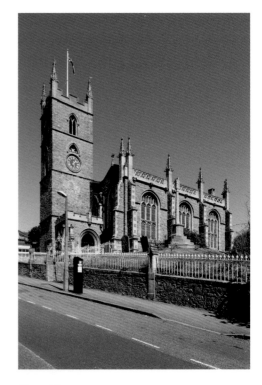

Figure 11
This modern view of Weston's parish church, St John the Baptist, shows that after it was reconstructed in 1824–5, the building was extended and enlarged in stages during the remainder of the 19th century.
[DP218539]

summer months. A decade later, Weston boasted 350 inhabited houses and only 25 uninhabited ones. The population had risen by 60 per cent to 2,103 in 1841, a rapid expansion compared to England's growth of 15 per cent, but actually broadly in line with the growth of other seaside resorts.

The 1838 tithe map is the first detailed map of Weston-super-Mare.[35] It shows that most of the High Street had been built on, the exception being the stretch on the west side, now occupied by the Italian Gardens. South Parade had been created, as had the south side of West Street. The triangular area at the junction between Meadow Street and Regent Street was beginning to be filled in. To the south of Regent Street was an area of dense housing (small dwellings that were home to artisans and tradesmen), but the seafront Beach Road was already occupied by much larger detached and semi-detached villas. Development at this date had spread as far as the north side of the future Ellenborough Park and the general grid pattern of streets was beginning to form in this area.

To the north-west of the village, where once the Revd William Leeves's thatched cottage had stood almost alone, Shepherd's Cottage was demolished and replaced in 1831 by 1–2 Beachfield Villas, built by Thomas Harrill (Fig 12). In 1838–41 the Victoria Buildings were constructed; the southern two, which have been least altered and are consequently listed, were built soon after the map was surveyed (Fig 13). On the slopes of Worlebury Hill an occasional detached villa had begun to appear and three houses could have been seen on what is now Grove Lane.

A directory and a guidebook published in 1840 recorded the steady progress being made.[36] Instead of five schools, there were now seven, and there were two libraries: Richard Hill's original library being run by Samuel Serle and the more recent one created by Joseph Whereat at the assembly rooms. The frequency of coach and waggon services increased during the decade and as the number of houses had grown, the number of lodgings similarly rose. The chancel of the parish church was rebuilt and enlarged in 1837 due to money provided by Archdeacon Henry Law (1797–1884), rector of the church from 1834 to 1838 and from 1840 to 1862.

The steady progress made during the early 19th century was creating a large village welcoming affluent visitors. However, Weston would begin to change dramatically from the 1840s onwards when the railway would make the growing town ultimately accessible to everyone.

Figure 12 (left)
1–2 Beachfield Villas are now part of the Lauriston Hotel, which was created through their amalgamation with the adjacent pair of Lauriston Villas.
[DP218412]

Figure 13 (above)
The Victoria Buildings formed the first terrace to be constructed on the seafront. Although originally built for wealthy residents, the houses were soon being used as lodgings for affluent holidaymakers. This photograph shows that most of the terrace has been raised by one storey.
[DP218275]

3

Victorian and Edwardian Weston-super-Mare

1841 and the future – Weston-super-Mare and the railway

The coming of the railway ushered in a period of rapid growth in the population of Weston-super-Mare, the number of tourists and the local industries. The middle decades of the 19th century witnessed a strong increase in the town's housing stock and saw the establishment of a standard form of Weston house, the two-storey, semi-detached or detached house constructed in local stone, but with oolitic limestone (Bath stone) detailing. The arrival of the railway also created distinct social zones in the town, with wealthy residents and their seasonal lodgers occupying the slopes up to Worlebury Hill and along the seafront, while the working-class population and holidaymakers with a limited budget occupied areas of dense housing beside the railway station and along the railway line. The latter location was also where larger-scale industry began to develop, including the town's renowned potteries. The coming of the railway effectively marks Weston-super-Mare's transition from a village to a town.

The Bristol and Exeter Railway Act 1836 authorised the creation of a railway line linking the two cities, a route that would pass close to Weston. However, there was initial local resistance to the railway, as some landowners felt it would be noisy and smoky, but the town relented and a short branch line was soon built to link it to the main line. Despite initial resistance and the consequent short delay, Weston became one of the first seaside resorts to enjoy a connection to the emerging national railway network when its station opened on 14 June 1841.

Initially, passengers were shuttled along the branch line in horse-drawn carriages, a journey that could take 30 minutes in bad weather. Weston's original station was on Alexandra Parade, roughly on the site of the former floral clock (*see* p 71), and disembarking visitors would have been greeted by the Railway Hotel, today's Tavern Inn, a facility constructed by Richard Parsley (*see* p 10). In 1847 it was described as 'a most convenient and desirable house for travellers' as 'it is within hearing of the bell announcing the departure of the trains, and possesses the accommodation of a daily ordinary'.[37] It had a billiard room and 'a very neat and commodious ASSEMBLY ROOM' capable of holding about 200 people, which was 'beautifully lighted up with gas, and as a concert

This 1920 Aerofilms photograph, taken from the south, shows the loop line of the railway at Weston-super-Mare and the branch line leading to the town's former passenger station (built in the 1860s) on the left. [EPW001031]

room is perhaps the best adapted for the purpose of any in the town'.[38]
On Sundays it was used as a Roman Catholic place of worship.

The impact of the railway was felt immediately. It was estimated in 1844 that some 23,000 visitors arrived by rail, an increase of around 300 per cent on the figures for the end of the coaching era, only five years earlier. Joseph Whereat (*see* p 20), the founder and editor of the *Weston-super-Mare Gazette*, recorded in 1845:

> Our town is fast enlarging and improving. The past few months have made very many additions to the number and neatness of its shops, and greater accommodation in every way is being provided for visitors. We think there is every reason to believe that the fears entertained by many that the Bristol and Exeter Railway would carry the usual visitors of Weston past us into Devonshire are likely to prove quite groundless. Weston-super-Mare is found to be just at the most convenient distance from Bristol and Bath, so that gentlemen can easily bring their families hither, and come and return by early and late Trains without any interruption of their usual hours of business.[39]

As well as individuals purchasing tickets, the ease of access to Weston-super-Mare led to the provision of organised excursions. On 2 June 1849, 1,600 workers from the Great Western Cotton Factory in Bristol assembled at the works at 6am and marched carrying banners and playing music to the railway station, where they boarded a train consisting of 16 carriages. On their arrival at Weston, the procession re-formed and marched through the town towards Birnbeck, 'where the party broke up and dispersed in various directions – some taking to the field, others to the sands, and others again to boating in the channel'.[40] After spending the day at Weston, the group assembled again in the evening at Knightstone and processed back to the station.

In 1851 the horse-drawn carriages on the branch line were replaced by steam power. A decade later a separate goods station and its short branch line were constructed behind where the Odeon Cinema now stands (on the corner of Walliscote Road and Regent Street). This new station proved particularly beneficial for the nearby Royal Pottery on Locking Road. By 1861 there was also 'a large and commodious room in the Locking-road for the accommodation of the excursion visitors'.[41] A new larger passenger station opened on 20 July 1866 and consisted of two platforms, a separate excursion platform and a refreshment hall.

Despite having a new station, Weston-super-Mare was still simply at the end of a branch line (Fig 14). In 1875 the Bristol and Exeter Railway (B&ER) tracks had been converted to standard gauge and this immediately opened up a wider, direct tourist market, the first excursion from Birmingham taking place on 18 July 1875. In the following year the B&ER amalgamated with the Great Western Railway, the combined company taking the GWR name. The same Act of Parliament behind the switch to standard gauge included a provision for the

Figure 14
Coinciding with the new station, a new signal box for the branch line was constructed, though it now stands unused, with its windows boarded up. It is said to be the oldest surviving signal box on the British rail system.
[DP218288]

creation of a loop line at Weston and therefore the present station was designed in 1875–6 by Francis Fox (1818–1914), the chief engineer for the B&ER, before its amalgamation with the GWR. However, there were significant delays, so the station finally opened for passengers on 1 March 1884. Additional capacity was provided at the turn of the 20th century, when a long excursion platform stretching from Alexandra Parade was constructed. It does not appear on an 1898 map but is present on a 1907 one. With the opening of the new station (Fig 15), the old passenger station that opened in 1866 was converted into a goods station, which closed in the 1960s, as did the excursion platform. This was a reflection of changing tourist habits, the car now being the dominant means of going on holiday. The site of the former goods station is now a supermarket (Fig 16).

Figure 15 (below)
Weston's current railway station is relatively small, with only two platforms flanking the twin tracks. [DP218284]

Figure 16 (right)
This extract from the 1886 Ordnance Survey map shows the 1860s railway station at the top of the map, disused by this date, beside Alexandra Parade, with the adjacent goods station. These were opposite the Town Hall, on the site of the Odeon Cinema, and the adjacent modern supermarket. To the south-east is the current station.

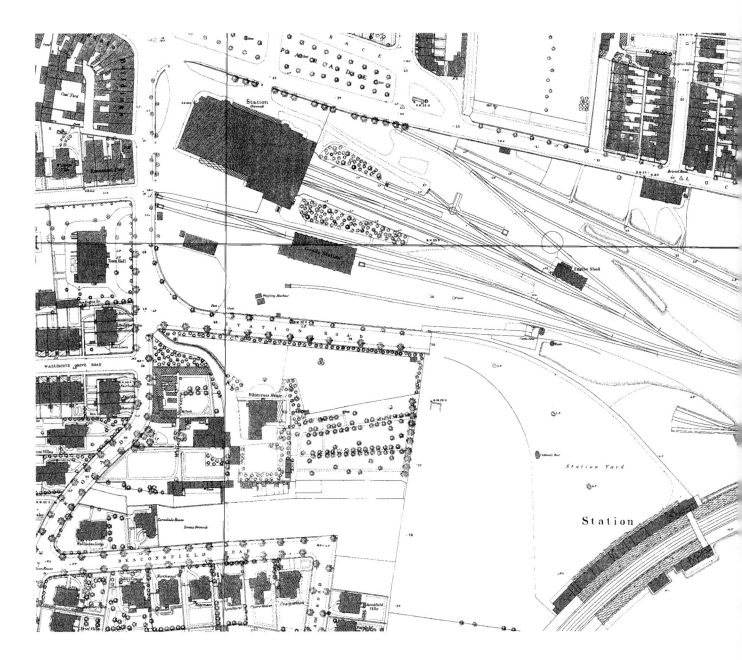

Governing Weston, 1841–1939

When the railway arrived in 1841, Weston-super-Mare was a settlement of just over 2,000 people, but a decade later, it had almost doubled in size to just over 4,000 residents. The village was becoming a town, and beginning to provide its residents and visitors with the first services. This required a move away from parochial administration to a more comprehensive form of local government.

An Improvement Act was obtained in 1842 for 'paving, lighting, watching, cleansing and otherwise improving the Town of Weston-super-Mare in the County of Somerset and for establishing a Market therein'.[42] This standard form of legislation created a wholly new local government structure based on a body of 18 Improvement Commissioners, leading figures in the town who were initially volunteers, but were subsequently elected. They were empowered to levy rates and borrow money to make improvements and compulsorily purchase land. For fire-safety reasons, thatched roofs were banned in all new properties, front doors of properties had to open inwards, and gutters and downpipes became compulsory. The Improvement Commissioners were also given powers to take down ruins and dangerous buildings and to remove any problematic projections and obstructions caused by buildings. They also controlled and licensed hackney carriages, and had a duty to regulate weights and measures. Their powers also included managing public nuisances, ranging from dung heaps and discarded fish to loitering prostitutes and people exposing themselves, and they also had duties concerning the welfare of animals. Two police officers were appointed, which was insufficient for a town receiving substantial influxes of trippers.

Henry Davies (1807–68), a local solicitor, was appointed as Clerk to the Commissioners and he went on to combine his legal practice with this new position. He was also a successful building speculator, his ventures including Oriel Terrace and Royal Crescent. He was at the centre of a later controversy about the Town Hall, as it was suggested that he as landowner was profiting from its construction.

The first meeting of Weston's Improvement Commissioners took place on 7 May 1842 in a meeting room at the gasworks in Oxford Street. Subsequently, they met at the Plough Hotel, but this was felt to be beneath the dignity of the institution. Therefore, in 1848 Francis Hutchinson Synge, first chairman of the

Improvement Commissioners, purchased the old Wesleyan chapel off the High Street. It could hold approximately 200 people, and was arranged so it could stage concerts as well as court hearings. However, it is clear that it was only expected to be a temporary measure and by the mid-1850s the need for a new town hall had been recognised. A competition for its design was held in 1856 and as a result of the generosity of Archdeacon Henry Law (1797–1884; *see* p 23) the new building was inaugurated on 3 March 1859. It contained the main hall, a smaller, though still large room for the Improvement Commissioners' meetings, as well as rooms for magistrates' meetings, police offices and cells for prisoners (Fig 17). The Petty Sessions was held fortnightly at the Town Hall, while the County Court met there monthly.

The growth of Weston-super-Mare during the second half of the 19th century meant the town outgrew its local government structures in stages. To coincide with the move into the new Town Hall in 1859, the Improvement Commissioners became the Board of Health for the whole district and in 1894 Weston became an Urban District Council. The increase in the town's population

Figure 17
The new Town Hall was constructed by James Wilson of Bath, at a cost of £3,000. It was enlarged and remodelled in 1897, at a cost of about £5,000, by Hans Price to include new offices and a council chamber for the recently created Urban District Council.
[DP218372]

was accompanied by the growing complexity of local government; there was simply more for local authorities to regulate and manage and therefore more sophisticated governance and a larger town hall was required. The original building was enlarged in 1897, and in 1909 a new committee room was added. The Town Hall was again extended, to the north, in 1927 by the architects Fry, Paterson & Jones, with the borough surveyor, Harold Brown. The parish of Milton was incorporated into Weston-super-Mare in 1902, and the civil parishes of Uphill and Worle followed suit in 1933. In 1937 Weston-super-Mare received its royal charter and quarry owner and developer Henry Butt (1861–1944; *see* p 106) became the first mayor of the borough. In 1974, under the Local Government Act 1972, Weston-super-Mare Borough Council was merged into the Woodspring District of Avon County Council. When Avon was split up in 1996, Weston became the administrative headquarters of the unitary authority of North Somerset.

As local government grew in size and complexity, and Weston-super-Mare's population increased, a number of the functions that had been accommodated within the Town Hall began to be housed in separate buildings. By the 1880s the police occupied a separate building in Oxford Street and in 1901 the fire brigade moved to a new two-storey fire station nearby.

The growth of Victorian Weston

Like other Victorian towns, Weston's population increased significantly during the 19th century and the town expanded, with new streets, houses, churches and schools being built. When the Census was enumerated in 1841, only 2,103 people lived in Weston; 60 years later, its population had grown nearly ten-fold to 19,018. The strongest growth happened during the 1840s and 1850s, when the population nearly doubled each decade. Thereafter, the growth rate slowed somewhat, but by 1911 the town was home to 23,235 people.

The growth in population is reflected in the number of houses in the town, which grew from 379 in 1841 to 3,094 in 1891. The strongest growth took place in the decade between 1851 and 1861, when the number of houses nearly doubled. The demand for housing was partially driven by the expansion of the permanent population and partly by the need to provide accommodation for seasonal visitors. Weston's railway connection to Bristol also meant it became effectively a prestigious marine suburb for Bristolians.

The construction of houses was the town's largest industry and descriptions in guidebooks and newspapers frequently commented on the rate of construction and change. In 1849 an astonished reporter described 'the various new rows, terraces, villas &c ... which grow while we gaze!'[43] And Robert Landemann Jones (c 1816–1903), the chairman of the local Master Builders' Association, opined that while Sheffield was remarkable for its cutlery and Manchester for its cotton, Weston was famous for its building activity: 'And well it may be, for within the memory of men now living its roads, esplanades, terraces, parks, and places have risen upon the sand tots of a wild and barren coast, occupied by a few poor fishermen, and the resort only of the sandpiper, the gulls and the curlew.'[44]

The development pattern of Weston's Victorian housing

At the beginning of Queen Victoria's reign, in 1837, most buildings in Weston were clustered around the High Street and along the seafront between Regent Street and Carlton Street. Development spread during the 1840s along the seafront towards Knightstone Island and further along towards Birnbeck Island. During the 1850s, several fashionable and exclusive hillside estates were developed, including the Shrubbery Estate and the Montpelier Estate. At the same time, development started to the south of the historic centre, including the roads around Ellenborough Park. These grand developments were aimed at prosperous citizens, wealthy retirees and visitors who wanted good-quality lodgings. In contrast, modest cottages and terraces for the lower classes were built close to the railway line, in the town centre and in the triangle framed by Meadow Street and Locking Road.

In the mid-19th century, prestigious developments in Weston-super-Mare tended to take the form of more or less grand terraces and crescents. The first examples were Victoria Buildings (1838–41), Albert Buildings (1843) and Princes Buildings (c 1843), all of which were relatively plain terraces of two- or three-storey houses. More ambitious were Oriel Terrace and Royal Crescent of 1847, both developments designed by architect James Wilson for Henry Davies (*see* p 32) on a strip of glebe land (Fig 18). They are faced in oolitic limestone (Bath stone) and Bath's architecture was clearly the inspiration for the latter, in name and form. Grand terraces and crescents continued to be built during the following decades: Wellington Terrace (1849; now 1–9 Upper Kewstoke Road), Manilla Crescent (1851), Ellenborough Crescent (1855), Royal Terrace (1860) and Claremont Crescent (1865–7), its convex side facing the sea. Most of these early schemes were built along the seafront, but the grand terrace reached its apogee with the two impressive Atlantic Terraces of 1859–61 on either side of Holy Trinity Church, high up on the hillside (Fig 19).

These isolated set pieces were soon overtaken in numbers and prevalence by large-scale villa developments on entire estates, which were built throughout the Victorian period and beyond. Villas, both semi-detached and detached, formed the characteristic building type of Weston. Initially, they were the preserve of the wealthiest inhabitants and could be found on the seafront and especially in estates on the slopes of Worlebury Hill. Early examples of grand villas include Villa Rosa in Shrubbery Road, and the semi-detached Elizabethan Villas in Birnbeck Road, both of 1844. Often these early examples were built in generous gardens, such as those of the first phase of development in the Shrubbery, but as development gathered pace whole streets of villas were

Figure 18 (above)
This Aerofilms photograph of 1930, taken from the east, shows Royal Crescent, with Oriel Terrace behind. Both were built in 1847 to a design by James Wilson of Bath for the solicitor Henry Davies.
[EPW033277]

Figure 19 (left)
The architect Henry Lloyd of Bristol designed the group of Holy Trinity Church and the flanking Atlantic Terraces as an architectural set piece on the hillside, which would be visible from the town centre. This aerial photograph, taken from the south-west, shows them in 2018.
[NMR 33488/023]

built. As the second half of the 19th century progressed, smaller versions were built in developments aimed at the middle classes, such as at the southern end of the Whitecross Estate.

The architecture of Victorian Weston appears particularly homogeneous due to its use of local, grey, carboniferous limestone, which was too hard to shape and was generally used in rockfaced blocks. A softer oolitic limestone (Bath stone) was frequently used for elaborate carvings and dressings that adorn even fairly standard Victorian semi-detached houses.

Weston's architects

The architect who left the strongest mark on the streetscape of Weston-super-Mare was Hans Fowler Price (1835–1912). When he moved to the town in 1860, there were few local architects and major commissions were given to outside architects as a matter of course. Soon he dominated the architectural scene to such an extent that other local architects of any stature only began to emerge at the end of the century when available work exceeded his practice's capacity and his career was drawing to a close.

Architects working in Weston during the pre-Price era generally came from Bath, Bristol and London. The first major architect to work in Weston was James Wilson (1816–1900) of Bath, whose main patrons in the area were Thomas Tutton Knyfton of Uphill Castle (now Uphill Manor) and Henry Davies. In 1841 Wilson was commissioned to build a new church in Uphill, which was followed by major alterations and additions to Uphill Castle in the 1850s, including a castellated gate lodge. In Weston-super-Mare, Wilson designed Oriel Terrace and the Royal Crescent for Davies in 1847 and the new Town Hall in 1856–9. Wilson also designed several villas at Weston, including Villa Rosa, a villa for a Mr Kerslake and a house for Davies on the Whitecross Estate.

Other architects only received isolated commissions in Weston-super-Mare. Those with more than one-off work included Manners & Gill, the practice of the Bath city architect George Phillips Manners (1789–1866), who designed the first two Anglican daughter churches in the town, Emmanuel Church and Christ Church (*see* Fig 33). Henry Lloyd of Bristol designed several major buildings during the 1850s–1860s, including Manilla Crescent, the assembly

rooms of 1858–9, and Holy Trinity and the Atlantic Terraces in 1859–61
(*see* Figs 19 and 34). In about 1849, William Christie of London built Victoria
Crescent, a group of semi-detached villas in Madeira Road, and Wellington
Terrace in nearby Upper Kewstoke Road. Gabriel & Hirst of Bristol extended
the Royal Hotel in 1849 (*see* Fig 5) and built the adjacent Royal Terrace.

Sometimes an architectural competition brought an architect from further
afield to Weston. Such competitions were held for many major buildings,
including the Independents' chapel of 1858 (Pritchett & Son of Darlington)
and the Victoria Methodist Church of 1899–1900 by W J Morley (1847-1930)
of Bradford.

Hans Fowler Price (1835–1912)

Buildings designed by Hans Price profoundly shaped Weston-super-Mare's
appearance. The architect was responsible for most houses and public buildings
erected in the town during the second half of the 19th century and the early
20th century (Fig 20). He is said to have completed about 861 projects between
1860 and his death in 1912, most of which were in Weston-super-Mare.

Figure 20 (left)
The striking furniture warehouse in Station Road was designed by Price & Jane in 1904 for the auctioneers and estate agents Messrs Lalonde Bros & Parham, who opened it in February 1905 with a staff dinner.
[DP218368]

Figure 21 (opposite, top)
This portrait shows Hans Fowler Price (1835–1912), the architect who dominated Weston's architectural scene and influenced the town's Victorian development.
[North Somerset Library Service]

Figure 22 (opposite, bottom)
28 Waterloo Street (the tallest building in this photograph) was designed by Hans Price as his own office. It remained in use by his successor practice into the late 20th century.
[DP218744]

Price was born in Bristol on 11 June 1835, the sixth child of Elizabeth (1802–96) and George (1798–1865), a druggist. By the age of 15 Price had been articled to Thomas Denville Barry (1815/16–1905), a Liverpool-based architect who specialised in the design of cemeteries. Price's earliest known architectural designs included his unsuccessful entry for the Manchester Assize Court competition of 1859, as well as the successful designs for cemeteries in Oswestry and Bristol of 1860, the latter an enlargement of Arno's Vale Cemetery.

By January 1860, Price had moved to Weston and set up as an architect and surveyor (Fig 21). His first office was at 5 High Street but by July 1861 it had moved to 1 Sydenham Terrace. It was located close to the office of the solicitor Samuel Baker (1796–1875) at number 7, the solicitor of the Pigott family (*see* p 7) and Price's future father-in-law. In about 1874, Price's practice moved to 28 Waterloo Street, a building he had designed himself (Fig 22). Price married Jane Plaister Baker (1840–89) on 17 September 1862. They lived with their growing family of six daughters and two sons first at Tyn-y-Coed in Hill Road (now demolished) and from about 1898 at what is now 7 Trewartha Park (*see* Fig 30).

Price's career took off shortly after moving to Weston. His first known works there included the remodelling and extension of the Baptist Church in Wadham Street in 1862–4, now the Blakehay Theatre, and his first major public building was the Weston-super-Mare and East Somerset Hospital of 1864–5. He launched his specialism of residential developments by laying out the Upper Worthy Estate for the Smyth Pigott family (1862–3) and then designing 54 houses in Woolcott Park, Redland, Bristol (1863–4), together with the local architect James Adams Clark. Between 1864 and 1870 he also designed several buildings in Clevedon for Sir Arthur Hallam Elton. While Price is most closely associated with Weston, his work can be found all over Somerset but also as far afield as Shropshire, Herefordshire, Pembrokeshire, Gloucestershire and Sussex.

Price held numerous official posts in Weston that led to further commissions, but also helped him keep in touch with his works once completed. Most notably he was elected as a Town Commissioner in 1884–7. Other appointments included the posts of vice-president of the Hospital Committee, chairman of the Weston-super-Mare Gaslight Company's board of directors, and a director and auditor of the Weston-super-Mare Pier Company, for whom he built some structures on Birnbeck Pier (1884, 1897–8). He was also a founding trustee of the School of Science and Art, and designed its new building.

During his career, Price was in partnership at least four times. In his earliest known partnership with James Adams Clark, Price was the junior partner, but his name was put first in all his subsequent partnerships. Relatively little is known about Clark (fl 1849–76), with whom Price worked on the Woolcott Park development in Bristol.

In 1873–7 Price was in partnership with Matthias August Edward Grosholz (1851–78), a young German architect who lived and worked in England for only a few years before emigrating to New Zealand. Price's longest partnership, lasting from 1877 to 1900, was with Walter Hernaman Wooler (1853–1936), who came from Dewsbury in West Yorkshire. Wooler married Ellen Stanley Marshall (1857–1936) in about 1883 and they lived at The Chalet in South Road. The partnership's last known project is dated 1900 and Wooler appears to have retired shortly afterwards. He and his wife are buried in Milton Road Cemetery. From 1902 Price was in partnership with William Jane (1864–1918), who had served his articles with Pope & Paul of Bristol in 1881–4 and then worked as chief assistant to the borough engineer and surveyor at Reading. During World War I, Jane served in the Royal Engineers, rising to the rank of major. He died from his wartime wounds in April 1918.

Price worked until his death on 27 November 1912; he is buried in Milton Road Cemetery. His obituaries in the local press praised his business sense, reliability, astuteness, 'remarkable fund of vitality' and 'practically unerring judgement'.[45] After Price's death, Jane continued the practice initially on his own. He then joined the practice of Peter George Fry as Jane & Fry. Their successor practice became Fry, Paterson & Jones and later Coffin, Jones & Roden, who were still based in Price's Waterloo Street office in 1979. They were bought out in the early 1990s by the firm Brittain Hadley and the practice was dissolved in 1997.

Price designed many of Weston's best-known public buildings, including the hospital, the sanatorium, the School of Science and Art, the former library and museum on the Boulevard, the current museum, several former church schools, and two council schools in Walliscote Road (*see* Fig 44) and Locking Road. Other major buildings, like the Victoria Hall in the Summer and Winter Gardens, and the Market Hall, no longer survive. Many of his public buildings, such as the library and the Walliscote Road schools, have highly decorative elevations. Indeed, for the School of Science and Art such decoration was an

Figure 23
The high costs of carvings and other decorations meant that the fine street elevation of the School of Science and Art could only be added seven years after the main building had been completed. [DP218737]

important display of the high standards in design it hoped to foster (Fig 23). The school's elevation featured faience panels and carvings by J P Steele of Kingsdown, Bristol. When it was finally completed in 1900, seven years after the main building opened, the *Weston Mercury* exclaimed, 'Happily barren ugliness has now given way to well-proportioned beauty.'[46]

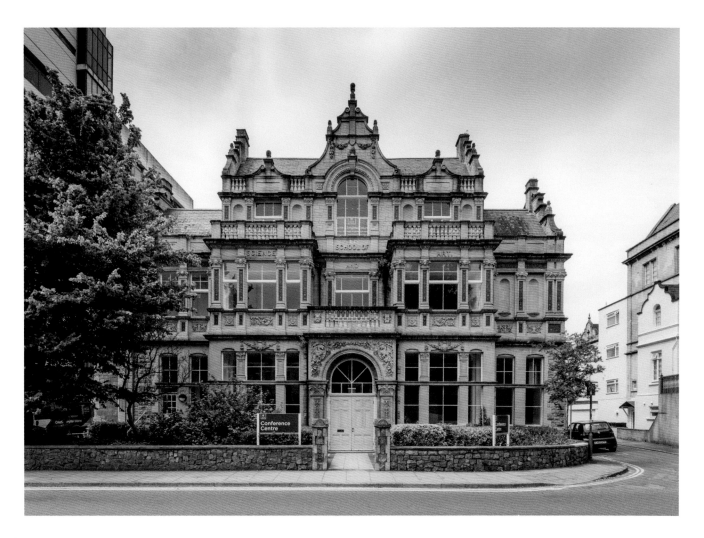

However, the vast majority of his oeuvre were private houses, supplemented by commercial, ecclesiastical and industrial commissions. He was involved in the layout and design of many estates in Weston-super-Mare, including the Milton Park Estate, the Upper Worthy Estate, the Montpelier Estate, the National Freehold Land Society Estate, the Sunnyside Estate, the Shrubbery Estate, the Whitecross Estate, the Coombe Bank Estate and the Swiss Villa Estate.

Price and the 'Weston style'

Apart from the prevalence of the local building materials, the town's architectural coherence also depended on a recognisable style of villa architecture, which was largely developed by Price. While this inevitably relied on a certain formula, it could also be lively in character. This was highlighted in the *Daily Graphic* in August 1891, which stated that 'monotony [in architecture] as in other seaside towns has no existence in Weston'.[47]

In general, Price and his practice worked in an eclectic style. His designs drew on many sources in their detailing, including Italianate, Gothic, Renaissance and Tudor. The Mercury Offices, for example, displays influences from Dutch Renaissance buildings, such as Leiden Town Hall, and Spanish churches, such as Segovia Cathedral. At the same time, Price's buildings, and in particular his villas, are generally instantly recognisable and appear to have influenced others, leading to the establishment of a 'Weston style'. Villas by Price generally have at least one gable to the main elevation that features some kind of decoration (Fig 24). This is typically a panel of carved stone in the earlier buildings, but might also be a carved bargeboard, or even tile-hanging after about 1900. It is not always possible to distinguish between works by Price or one of his partners. Wooler, in particular, is credited occasionally with sole authorship, although hard evidence is frequently lacking. The Weston formula was not in any way revolutionary, but its prevalence, together with the widespread use of local stone combined with Bath stone dressings, gave Victorian Weston a distinct visual identity that was not simply derivative of urban and suburban residences in Bristol or Bath.

Figure 24
This example of a decorative gable shows one of Hans Price's houses in Beaconsfield Road, which combines several Jacobean-style motifs, such as strapwork and a carved shell.
[DP218345]

Wilde & Fry

Other notable architects emerged towards the end of the 19th century, in particular Sydney John Wilde (born 1852), who formed a partnership with his former assistant Peter George Fry (1875–1925). Wilde's best-known works were the Commercial Cable Company office of 1889–90 in Richmond Street (*see* Fig 59) and the former St Saviour's church of 1890–92 in Locking Road.

Fry was articled to Wilde between 1891 and 1895, and three years later they formed a partnership that lasted until 1909. Wilde & Fry collaborated on several occasions with Price, notably on the library and museum in the Boulevard. Fry's main work was St Paul's Anglican Church of 1911–12. After 1912, Fry went into partnership with Price's last partner, William Jane. After Jane's death, Fry formed a new partnership with Paterson and Jones, creating Fry, Paterson & Jones, which continued until the 1960s. Major works by Fry, Paterson & Jones include the town hall extension of 1927 and the Victoria Methodist Church of 1935–6 in Station Road.

Weston's estates

Smyth Pigott Estate

A number of estates shaped the development of large swathes of Weston-super-Mare. The largest estate was owned by the Smyth Pigott family and comprised the northern part of the town and much of the fashionable hillside. Gradually it released land for development, the earliest known building leases being in Wadham Street and dating from 1846. The estate experienced three distinct peaks of development: in the late 1850s (South Road and Upper and Lower Church Road), the early 1870s (George Street and Bristol Road) and the late 1890s and early 1900s (Hatfield Road, Hughenden Road and Milton Road). However, perhaps the estate's most significant contribution to Weston's townscape was the creation in the 1860s of the Boulevard and its continuation Waterloo Street as a link to the Montpelier Estate (Fig 25). North of the Boulevard and east of the Pigotts' Grove House was the Grove Town development, with Landemann Circus at its heart. Other discrete entities were the development of the Upper Worthy Estate, just to the east of Grove Park, during the early 1860s, the Torfield during the 1870s and Grove Park Road in the 1890s.

Apart from the Pigott family, two people shaped the development of the Smyth Pigott Estate: Robert Landemann Jones and Hans Price. Jones (*see* p 35) was the land agent and steward for the Smyth Pigott Estate. He had a varied early career, including in the Merchant Navy, but was in the employ of the Pigotts by the early 1850s. A tribute accompanying his obituary quoted his motto that 'the interests of the Pigott estates and those of the town are not only identical but inseparable, and together they must stand or fall'.[48] He was one of the promoters of the sanatorium, brought the 'Italian Band' to the town at his own expense, and supported many public schemes such as the waterworks (1854) and the Summer and Winter Gardens (1882–4).

Hans Price was the estate's consulting architect and surveyor from at least 1862. He was also connected to the estate by his marriage to the daughter of the Smyth Pigotts' solicitor, although it is not known whether he achieved his position through his marriage or met his wife through his work. Price designed

Figure 25
This photograph of 1888 shows the view to the west along the Boulevard and Waterloo Street, with the recently planted trees lining the street.
[North Somerset Library Service]

many of the new houses for the Smyth Pigott family, including the Upper Worthy Estate (laid out in 1862), 67 cottages in Grove Town in 1871 and 19 houses in Grove Park Road in 1891–6.

Whitecross Estate

The second-largest estate was Richard Parsley's Whitecross Estate in the southern part of the town. A few years after Parsley's death in 1846, his son Horatio sold most of its land to Henry Davies and Joseph Whereat (*see* p 20). They promptly held an architectural competition, which was won by William Bonython Moffatt (1812–87) of London. Moffatt's winning scheme was a plan for 500 houses and an Anglican church on the 200-acre site. The houses were clearly aimed at the wealthy and upper-middle classes, with plot sizes ranging from a quarter of an acre to an acre. The first part to be realised was Ellenborough Crescent (1855–6), followed by Ellenborough Park (Fig 26). They were named after Edward Law (1790–1871), first Earl of Ellenborough, politician and Governor-General of India, and cousin of Archdeacon Henry Law, the rector of Weston.

Figure 26
Ellenborough Park and Ellenborough Crescent were the first developments on the Whitecross Estate, to the south of the town. and their houses were aimed at wealthy residents. This aerial photograph was taken from the south-west.
[NMR 33489/053]

The deaths of Wheat in 1865 and Davies in 1868 halted these grand plans and the southern part of the estate remained undeveloped for another 20 years. Davies's widow, Rebecca, kept the central part of the estate but sold 16 acres to the east to William Morgan of Bath; this later became the Sunnyside Estate (*see* p 51). In 1882 Rebecca Davies donated Clarence Park as a public park and the neighbouring streets were built up soon after (Fig 27). The bulk of this part of the estate was developed during the 1880s by the British Land Company, the subsidiary of the National Freehold Land Society (*see* p 49). Instead of grand houses for the most affluent, the society's members built smaller houses aimed at a less wealthy market.

Shrubbery Estate and Coombe Bank Estate

The Shrubbery Estate, also known as the 'Villa Rosa Estate' after its most prominent villa, was one of the most exclusive of the early residential developments. Sophia Rooke (1787–1874) acquired the land during the 1830s and later started the residential development. In 1844 she commissioned James Wilson of Bath to design a grand Italianate residence of pink limestone, called the Villa Rosa. It was built on the site of an earlier house, which in 1838 was inhabited by the Irish author Lady Eliza Tuite (*c* 1764–1850). This was followed by three further villas, called Overcoombe (1850, by Robert Ebbels of Wolverhampton), Coombe Bank and Coombe Cottage, subsequently renamed Coombe Lodge. These houses and the Villa Rosa were surrounded by the landscape of the 'shrubbery' (Fig 28). A south lodge of 1839 guarded the entry to the estate and a north lodge followed in 1871; other lodges were created as staff accommodation. The second phase of development started in around 1859 and was more intensive, although still consisting of generously sized villas in large grounds. A network of winding roads was laid out (Fig 29), reflecting the sinuous paths of the previous landscaping on much of the site. In 1859 a plan showing 30 pairs of semi-detached villas was drawn up by J P Sturge & Sons, surveyors of Bristol. A well and a castellated water tower, now in residential use, supplied the estate. Communal gardens, known as 'Shrubbery Walks', were provided, just to the south of the water tower.

A third phase of development, starting after Sophia Rooke's death, was even denser, encroaching on the gardens of the Villa Rosa and Coombe Cottage.

Figure 27 (above)
This plaque commemorates Rebecca Davies's gift of Clarence Park in 1882 in memory of her husband, Henry. Her gift had stipulated that games should be restricted to the eastern half and in her later years she fought any attempts to encroach on free public access to the western half.
[DP218573]

Figure 28 (opposite)
This map shows the Shrubbery Estate in 1853, with four villas in the southern half of the eponymous landscaped gardens, as well as a lodge at the south and the gardener's lodge at the northeast.
[North Somerset Library Service]

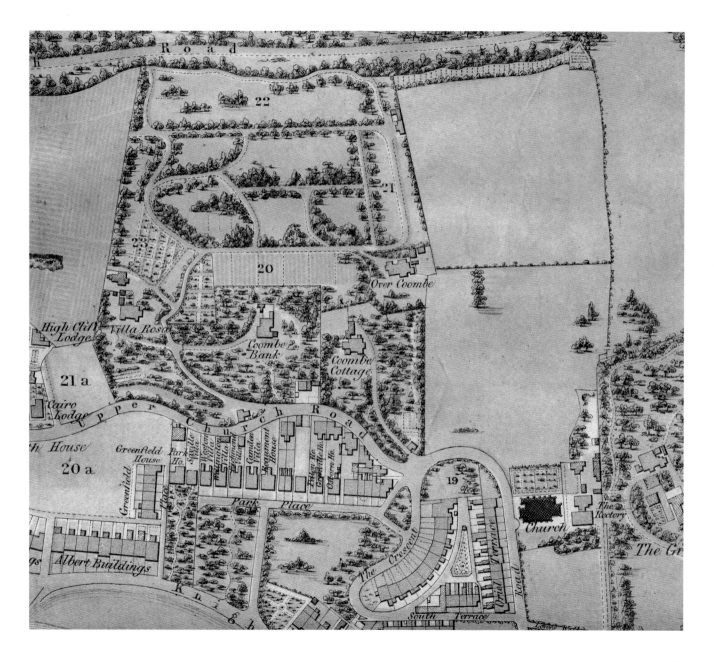

To the north of Villa Rosa, Shrubbery Terrace was built in about 1877.
At the same time, Hans Price designed nine pairs of semi-detached villas and
five detached villas, grouped around Coombe Bank House. This process of
densification continued in the Edwardian period, when Victoria Park was
laid out on the site of Coombe Cottage.

Montpelier Estate

The fashionable Montpelier Estate, to the north-east of the town centre, was
started by Henry Davies during the late 1850s. He had bought the land in 1852
and Joseph White's town plan of the following year shows an initial unrealised
layout with an oval reservoir. Drainage plans were prepared in 1856 and
building started soon after, focusing on the west side of Montpelier. As in the
Shrubbery Estate, water supply was an essential facility and a reservoir was built
at the north end of the street in 1854. Another important amenity was the
construction of Christ Church in 1854–5; Davies donated the site and funds
towards its construction (*see* Fig 33). In 1863 Thomas Beedle described
Montpelier as 'handsome and healthy ... one of the modern beauties of
Weston'.[49] Price was involved in the later phases; he designed several villas
on the east side of Montpelier during the 1870s.

Not all of the estate was developed by Davies himself. In 1858 he sold a plot
located south of the junction of Montpelier and Hill Road to Thomas Morland
and Conrad Wilkinson, trustees of the National Freehold Land Society. The form
of any development was regulated by strict covenants, ensuring the quality and
appearance was consistent with Davies's own development on adjoining plots.
This development, as well as that on an adjoining site in Hill Road, was aimed at
the wealthy and upper-middle-class market and demonstrates that the society
had left its origins in the electoral franchise movement long behind and had
become a mainly commercial proposition. By contrast, the society's development
south of Milton Road, untrammelled by cost and quality restrictions, was denser
and of smaller villas (*see* p 49).

By the 1880s the east side of Montpelier was largely built up, including
the large house called Trewartha at the north and a D-shaped street called
Montpelier East (now part of Trewartha Park). The northern half of Trewartha
Park was added during the late 1890s, and Price designed four pairs of semi-
detached houses (Fig 30).

Figure 29
*Shrubbery Road, at the centre of the Shrubbery Estate,
bisected the gardens of the Villa Rosa, prompting the
construction of a bridge to link the two halves.
[DP218585]*

Figure 30
In the late 1890s, Hans Price designed a group of
semi-detached houses in Trewartha Park. Number 7,
pictured here, was to be his own house, where he lived
with his family until his death in 1912.
[DP218504]

Swiss Villa Estate

Not every projected housing development was successful. Several proposals for the area around Swiss Villa, to the south of Montpelier, were delayed or failed to materialise, partly due to its poor location. It was inland, without a sea view and close to the railway, the cattle market and Locking Road. Swiss Villa existed by 1838 and is best known for Isambard Kingdom Brunel's reputed stay there in 1841. White's 1853 map shows a first proposal for three streets of villas framing Swiss Villa, which was then owned by the solicitor Joseph Edgar. This remained unexecuted, as did Edgar's scheme to build cottages based on John Nash's Blaise Hamlet near Bristol, although one cottage was described in an 1854 guidebook.[50]

A more successful attempt to develop the land was made during the late 1870s. In 1879 tenders were invited to build a main drain for the estate and work started at the west with the construction of the west side of Swiss Road. The eastern part of the estate had been built by 1903. A second phase of development was initiated in the early 1900s by the Cox family, who demolished Swiss Villa and sold the land. Between 1904 and 1907 Gordon Road, Milburn Road and Trevelyan Road were built over the site of the villa and its gardens. Overall, the character of the Swiss Villa Estate was closer to the medium-sized houses of the Freehold Land Estate to its north, rather than the large villas of the Montpelier Estate that the initial scheme of the early 1850s had tried to emulate.

Middle-class Victorian and Edwardian housing

Other developments were aimed at the middle classes, although the exact socio-economic market is not always easy to ascertain. There were several developments by the National Freehold Land Society (NFLS) and its commercial subsidiary, the British Land Company. While the widening of the electoral franchise through property ownership had been a founding principle of the society, the NFLS quickly became a commercial operation and its houses were aimed at people more affluent than the poorest in society. The plots were distributed by ballot among the members, based on the number of shares they held. The members were generally free to build in whatever style or plan they chose, or even to leave the plot fallow for some years.

By 1858 the NFLS owned three plots of land. Two have already been mentioned, both sold by Henry Davies with covenants (*see* p 48). A third was located to the south of Milton Road, where houses were aimed at middle-class owners. This plot, encompassing Clarendon Road and parts of nearby Hill Road, Milton Road and Ashcombe Road, was acquired in about 1853. Development only started in earnest in about 1869 and continued into the 1880s, a typical example of the frequently piecemeal NFLS developments (Fig 31).

During the 1880s the British Land Company developed the southern part of the Whitecross Estate, including Clevedon Road, Clifton Road, Severn Road, Whitecross Road and Walliscote Road. These houses appear more homogenous

Figure 31
Clarendon Road was developed by the National Freehold Land Society between the late 1860s and the 1880s. Hans Price designed several cottages and villas in the street, as well as a corner shop.
[DP218647]

in appearance than the earlier NFLS development, albeit still a mixture of semis and terraces, and they appear to have been developed relatively soon after the plots were released. A small shopping centre was established in Whitecross Road, which soon spilled over from purpose-built shops into converted houses.

One of the investors who acquired plots from the British Land Company was local house decorator William R Palmer. He recounted in his memoirs that in 1889 he built two houses on adjacent plots on Severn Road, after allotments on the site proved a financial failure. Finding tenants also proved difficult and Palmer himself lived in one house for a time. His experience shows that houses proved a better investment opportunity than allotments but that the demand for houses to rent was not always strong.

The eastern part of the Whitecross Estate was sold by the Davies family to William Morgan of Bath. It was developed as part of the Sunnyside Estate by the ABC Syndicate, whose acronym was formed from the surnames of the three directors: Charles Addicott, a prominent local builder, Henry Butt, a quarry owner, merchant and future town mayor, and the ironmonger John Pitman Curtis. Between 1904 and 1912, Price designed numerous houses and roads for the estate. After much lobbying by the syndicate, a road bridge over the railway line was built in 1910, which linked Clevedon Road and Brighton Road, and the two halves of the estate on either side of the railway. On the west side of the railway, the estate was an infill development, extending the British Land Company's streets such as Clevedon Road to the east and connecting them with new streets on the other side of the railway line.

Another Edwardian development for less wealthy residents, which made use of land beside the railway line, was the Bournville Estate. In about 1904 the Poole family of Brislington developed Bournville Road. Mr Poole allegedly named the road after Cadbury's model village in Birmingham (laid out in 1895), probably to signal to potential buyers and tenants that this might be a similar model village. The earliest buildings took the form of a long terrace of houses. This was followed by Amberey Road to the north, again mostly with long terraces, and Kensington Road to the south from about 1909. The interwar years saw the first major expansion of this small estate, with a further expansion after 1945.

Working-class housing

Working-class housing developments took place in the vicinity of the railway station and the railway line. Initially, these were in the town centre, close to workplaces. During the 1850s and 1860s, terraces of small houses were built in a triangle formed by the railway station, Meadow Street and Orchard Street. This area expanded over the following decades but areas of lower-class housing were also increasingly found further afield. For example, in the early 1850s the terraces of 'Camden Town' were built in Locking Road, comprising two-storey cottages, which today are known as Camden Terrace, the southern end of George Street, and Little George Street (Fig 32).

Places of worship

Queen Victoria's reign saw a huge increase in Weston's population and a growth in the number of denominations worshipping in the town, factors prompting the construction of numerous places of worship. At the beginning of the 19th century, the only purpose-built places of worship in Weston, Worle and Uphill were the historic Anglican parish churches, but by the end of the century the major Christian denominations were well represented.

Anglican churches

Between 1837 and 1914, six new Anglican churches were built in Weston, as well as new churches in Milton and Uphill, and older churches were restored or replaced. The medieval church in Worle was restored and extended by John Norton (1822–1904) in 1869–70. Weston's historic parish church of St John the Baptist was extended several times during the century to keep up with the growth in population, although it was not full out of season. The north aisle was added in 1844, followed by the south aisle by Price & Wooler in 1890. Uphill's medieval church on the top of the hill was replaced in 1841–4 by a new building on a more convenient site but the old church was retained. The new church was extended in 1891–2.

The early Victorian foundations of Anglican churches and schools were due to the exertions of Archdeacon Henry Law (*see* p 23). Law not only

Figure 32
The cottages at the south end of George Street were built in the early 1850s, as part of a small working-class development called 'Camden Town'.
[DP218651]

initiated the building of three new churches and two schools, but also contributed financially to their construction and endowment. The first new church to open was Emmanuel Church in 1847, in Oxford Street. The church clearly fulfilled an urgent need; in March 1851 it had an estimated attendance of 310 for the morning service and 600 for the afternoon service and during the summer season attendance would have been even higher. The design of Emmanuel Church must have found favour with Archdeacon Law as the same architects, Manners & Gill, also received the commission for Christ Church, of 1854–5 (Fig 33). Christ Church is located picturesquely on the slopes of Montpelier, a district then under construction. It was extended in 1877 and heightened in 1889, when a clerestory was added, both by Price's practice.

The third new Anglican parish church was that of Holy Trinity, on Atlantic Road, in the suburb of what was then known as Cliftonville (Fig 34). The church, of 1859–61, formed the centrepiece of the two contemporary Atlantic Terraces, which were, like the church, designed by Henry Lloyd of Bristol. While under construction, a gale on 20 February 1861 blew down the spire, which collapsed into the nave. The completed church finally opened on 3 October 1861.

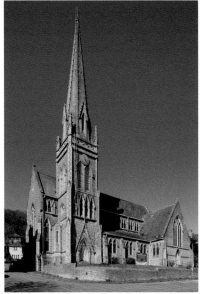

Figure 33 (left)
Christ Church of 1854–5 was one of the first buildings in the new district of Montpelier and its plot was donated by local landowner Henry Davies. This photograph was taken in around 1877, when the chancel extension by Price & Grosholz was under construction, with scaffolding visible at the right-hand side of the photograph.
[North Somerset Library Service]

Figure 34 (right)
Holy Trinity Church on Atlantic Road was the third Anglican church to be built during Victoria's reign. It served the new, exclusive suburb of Cliftonville, on the hillside.
[DP218552]

The next two Anglican churches were located on the outer fringe of the town: St Jude's Church, Milton (now St Andrew's Greek Orthodox Church) was built in 1885–7 to a Gothic design by Price & Wooler. St Saviour's, in Locking Road, was built in two stages in 1890–92 and 1901–2, but Sydney J Wilde's original design was never completed. It has been converted into flats.

In 1898 construction began on a permanent church dedicated to All Saints to replace an iron church of 1871. Designed by the leading church architect George Frederick Bodley (1827–1907), only the chancel (1898–9), the nave and the north aisle (1902) were completed during his lifetime. After his death, work continued to his design. Despite these piecemeal additions, John Betjeman thought it 'the finest church of entirely modern foundation in Somerset'.[51] The last Anglican church to be built before World War I was St Paul's of 1911–12, which replaced an iron church of 1897. It was designed by Peter George Fry (*see* p 40) in a neo-Perpendicular style but a planned tower was never completed. The church was hit by an air raid on 4 January 1941 (*see* Fig 83), and was restored in 1954–7 by Harold Jones of Fry, Paterson & Jones.

During the late 19th century, several Anglican parishes established mission halls or rooms to serve poor neighbourhoods. Such missions encouraged church and school attendance, but also provided basic welfare such as food and medicine. For example, Holy Trinity parish built a mission room off Manilla Crescent, while Christ Church had one in Alfred Street and a second one in Ashcombe Park Road.

Nonconformist and Catholic churches

Nonconformist groups in the Weston area had small beginnings but soon grew due to the influx of visitors and permanent residents. The earliest Nonconformists with a permanent base in the area were the Wesleyans, who had early chapels at Worle (1813) and Uphill (1841). In Weston itself, Methodist meetings were initially held in a converted cottage until a purpose-built Gothic chapel opened in 1847 at the corner of Regent Street and St James Street (Fig 35). On 30 March 1851, this chapel had the largest Nonconformist congregation in the town, with 290 attending in the morning and 360 in the evening. It was altered in 1860 and closed in 1899, then converted by Hans Price in 1901 into two houses with shops.

Figure 35
Shown in a print of around 1850, Regent Street was historically the primary route from the railway station to the seafront. The construction in 1847 of Weston's first purpose-built Methodist chapel on this route was an important statement of Nonconformist presence. [North Somerset Library Service]

REGENT STREET,
WESTON-SUPER-MARE

In 1857 the Wesleyan Association and the Methodist Reform Churches formed the United Methodist Free Churches, which built several churches in Weston. These included a chapel of 1866 in Burlington Street (Fig 36), as well as one by Price, which opened 10 years later at the corner of Orchard Street and the Boulevard. The Methodist Church of 1879–81 in Upper Church Road, by Alexander Lauder of Barnstaple (*c*1837–*c*1921), is a more elaborate Gothic building with a slim needle spire. Other Methodist chapels were located in Milton and in Hill Road. In 1907–8 the Primitive Methodists built a chapel and Sunday school in Brighton Road, designed by Wilde & Fry. But the grandest Methodist building in Weston was the Victoria Methodist Church of 1899–1900 in Station Road (Fig 37). It was designed in a Decorated Gothic style with a spire and large traceried windows. The architect was W J Morley of Bradford, who had won an architectural competition held in 1898. Methodists also established mission rooms and halls, including the 'iron room' on the west side of Orchard Street (Fig 38).

The Independent Chapel,
WESTON SUPER MARE

The Independents (later Congregationalists) arrived in Weston during the 1820s. In 1829 or 1830 they opened a chapel in the High Street, which had a portico with Ionic columns. In 1858 it was replaced by a Gothic chapel with a 30.5m-high steeple, by Pritchett & Son of Darlington (Fig 39). A new chapel in the Boulevard was built in 1875–6 to a design by T L Banks (1842–1920), with Sunday schools to the rear. The original chapel in the High Street became an ironmonger's shop. Another Congregational base was established in Moorland Road when a Sunday school was built there in 1894, followed by an iron chapel in 1904.

The first Baptist chapel in Weston was the Italianate chapel in Wadham Street, which opened in August 1850. By 1862 it had become too small for the congregation and it was decided to let Price enlarge the church to provide 400 additional seats (Fig 40). Price also designed the second Baptist chapel, a Gothic building of 1865–6 on the hillside in Lower Bristol Road, with an octagonal tower and spire. There was a further Baptist chapel in Worle, and in December 1908 a dual-purpose school and chapel opened in Walliscote Road, in an Arts-and-Crafts-influenced building by the architects Silcock & Reay.

Figure 36 (opposite, top left)
This modest chapel of 1866 in Burlington Street was one of many churches built by Methodists in the second half of the 19th century. It was later used by the Bible Christians.
[DP218735]

Figure 37 (opposite, bottom left)
The first Victoria Methodist Church in Station Road, shown in this early 20th-century photograph, burnt down in 1935 and was replaced by the present church.
[North Somerset Library Service]

Figure 38 (opposite, top right)
The Methodist mission room in Orchard Street had been built by 1886. It was later used as a shop and is now disused.
[DP218525]

Figure 39 (opposite, bottom right)
The Independents' Chapel of 1858 was originally in the High Street. When the congregation moved to the Boulevard in 1876, this was converted by Hans Price into an ironmonger's shop, and the spire was moved to the chapel of Banwell Abbey, around 5 miles east of Weston-super-Mare.
[North Somerset Library Service]

Figure 40 (right)
The former Baptist Church in Wadham Street, now the Blakehay Theatre, was built in 1850 and extended in 1862 by Hans Price.
[DP218538]

The Roman Catholic parish in Weston-super-Mare was founded in 1806. Initially, services were held in the Railway Hotel, but in 1858 St Joseph's Roman Catholic Church (Fig 41) was built on a site donated by Joseph Ruscombe Poole (died 1890), who also paid the architect Charles Hansom (1817–88) and the builder. John Hugh Smyth Pigott, who had converted to Catholicism, donated the stone. Hansom designed a small church, comprising a nave and chancel, which could be extended. This finally happened in 1893, to designs by the architect-priest Canon A J C Scoles (1844–1920).

By the 1880s there were three Plymouth Brethren halls in Weston and one in Worle; only the Waterloo Gospel Hall of 1876 by Price & Grosholz in Waterloo Street remains in use today. By 1886 the Exclusive Brethren were based in the Boulevard Rooms on the south side of the Boulevard, but by 1897 they had sold the building to the Baptists.

Figure 41
St Joseph's Roman Catholic Church of 1858 by Charles Hansom was the first purpose-built Catholic church in Weston.
[DP218486]

Quakers first met in private houses, but in 1846 Richard Parsley offered them a site in Union Street and the meeting house opened in that year, though the internal gallery was still unfinished in 1855. The building was destroyed by bombing in 1942 and a new meeting house was built on the site in two phases, which opened in 1953 and 1956. Other Victorian places of worship include the chapel in the sanatorium and the Salvation Army hall of 1882 in Carlton Street, which was replaced in 2002.

Educating Victorian and Edwardian Weston

Anglican church schools dominated the provision of education in Weston until the end of the 19th century. In 1835, the year after Archdeacon Law's arrival in Weston, he opened an infants' school at the east end of Carlton Street. Ten years later, in September 1845, the National School opened at the corner of Knightstone Road and Lower Church Road, again on the initiative of the rector (Fig 42). This was an expansion of the earlier parish school of 1822, which relocated here from 'the Batch' (now the site of 4–8 All Saints Road). The school

Figure 42
This photograph shows the National School of 1845. It closed in 1964 and Weston College was built on its site.
[North Somerset Library Service]

was to serve all children in Weston, including the seasonally employed donkey boys who had to rely on charity during the winter. The building was described on its opening as 'a plain Gothic structure, but neat and substantial, pleasantly and beautifully situated'.[52] In 1863 Christ Church parish school opened in Baker Street, in a building designed by Captain Tate. Demand was high and its capacity was frequently exceeded, prompting the building of extensions in 1873–4 and 1905. Parish schools were also built in Worle in 1865, which incorporated the remains of a medieval tithe barn, and in Uphill in 1872.

The first non-Anglican school was the British School in Hopkins Street, which opened in 1855, with space for 150 children (Fig 43). It was extended in 1887 to accommodate 335 children. Adult education also became an increasing concern. In 1846 the Mechanics Institute was opened by the Revd Joseph Hopkins, the minister of the Independent Chapel. By 1854, this was based in the temporary town hall building in the High Street, where meetings were held and lectures given, as well as winter classes in drawing, singing, arithmetic, English grammar and composition. In 1859 a night school was founded by Miss Salter in Carlton Street, which moved in 1863 to the Albert Memorial Hall, beside Emmanuel church.

In 1870 the new Elementary Education Act was passed, encouraging the building of schools by providing grants from central government. Where this was insufficient, it allowed the formation of school boards, whose members were elected by the ratepayers. As happened elsewhere, the Anglican parishes of Weston were keen to stave off the formation of such a board, which would have imposed non-denominational religious teaching, and therefore they redoubled their efforts to expand parish school places. When the British School nearly closed in the mid-1870s due to financial difficulties, the Anglicans supported it. However, demand for school places increasingly outstripped provision and in 1893 a school board with nine members was established. Hans Price was appointed architect to the board, a post he continued to hold after responsibility for education passed to Somerset County Council in 1903.

No expense was spared for the first school to be built by the board. A site in Walliscote Road was acquired for £6,042 12s, and the buildings, comprising a main block for boys and girls and a detached infants' block, cost £10,041. An architectural competition was held in November 1894 and a professional assessor, the eminent school architect E R Robson (1835–1917), was appointed

Figure 43
After its opening in 1855, the British School was described by the Taunton Courier and Western Advertiser *as a 'handsome, lofty, and well-ventilated building'.*
[DP218581]

after pressure on the board from the architectural press and establishment. Robson's choice of design was, however, overruled by the committee, who instead chose a design disqualified for violating the competition's conditions; controversially, this design was found to be by Price, the board's architect (Fig 44). The finished school was opened on 30 July 1897 by Sir George Kekewich, Permanent Secretary to the Department of Education. The old infants' school in Carlton Street was repurposed as 'a gymnasium and covered playground for the girls and infants'.[53]

The second board school, in Locking Road, was built to a more constrained budget and in a plainer style. The site cost £2,032 and the building £4,563, in total less than half of the cost of the Walliscote Road school. The first block, which opened in December 1899, was designed jointly by Hans Price and Sydney J Wilde, who also designed the girls' block six years later. A third board school was planned in 1902 for the Moorland Road area, to the south of the town centre, but nothing was built there before World War I. In 1906, a small infants' school, now Milton Park Primary School was built at Milton to a design by Price & Jane.

Figure 44
The Board School in Walliscote Road with its dramatic roofscape is one of Hans Price's best-known buildings and one of his most elaborately decorated.
[DP218258]

In parallel with the church and council schools, there was also a wide range of private schools. In 1855 there were nine such schools for 'ladies' and seven for 'gentlemen' and by 1914 there were at least 30.[54] As well as promising health benefits, it was fashionable to send children to a school by the sea. There were a few purpose-built private schools, but most of them were in converted houses and villas. In 1859 the College, a private boys' school founded in around 1846 by Jonathan Elwell in Sidmouth House, moved into grand new premises in Beach Road (Fig 45). When the school moved out in 1889, the building was enlarged and reopened as the Grand Atlantic Hotel (*see* Fig 68).

St Peter's Preparatory School for boys was founded in 1882 by the Revd Robert Duckworth. Based initially at Highbury in Atlantic Terrace East, it was aimed at boys preparing 'for the Universities, Army, Navy, the Public Schools &c'.[55] By 1884, the school occupied the three easternmost houses of the terrace,

The College, Weston Super Mare

Figure 45
This engraving shows the Beach Road premises of the College, one of Weston's many private schools, before the building was converted to the Grand Atlantic Hotel (see Fig 68).
[North Somerset Library Service]

Figure 46
The three-storey Arts-and-Crafts-influenced St Peter's
School, designed by the architects Ward & Cogswell,
was built in 1906. It had the master's house at one end,
the 'big school room' in the centre and the classrooms
at the other end.
[North Somerset Library Service]

as well as a two-storey extension built that year by Price & Wooler. In 1906 the school moved to a new building on a large site to the north of the parish church (Fig 46). The area to the south of the school included a recreation ground, tennis courts and a swimming pool. Its most famous alumnus was the writer Roald Dahl, who attended for four years in the 1920s. The school closed in 1970. Between around 1914 and 1934, its former building in Atlantic Terrace East was used by St Faith's School for girls.

Servicing the growing town

By the mid-19th century, towns were beginning to have the technology and the desire to provide their citizens with the first basic services, either through local government activity or through supporting an enterprising private company. Weston-super-Mare's first gasworks was erected in 1841 on land 'given for that purpose by R Parsley', and adjacent to it a new church was to be constructed, the future Emmanuel Church.[56] Initially 42 public lamps and about 50 private consumers were served and by 1847 the company was providing gas for 60 public lamps and a growing number of private consumers. An 1853 map of Weston-super-Mare shows two small gasholders and other buildings on the site, close to the new church and a dense area of working-class housing.

A gasworks does not seem to have been considered a hindrance to development in the 1840s, despite the noxious emissions and the regular influx of carts bringing coal and taking away coke. However, by 1854 a guidebook was complaining that the gasworks in Gas Street gave 'a dingy appearance to the neighbouring tenements, principally inhabited by the poor'.[57] If the town was to grow, a new company and a new site further out providing more gas was required and in 1856 a new, larger gasworks was created on Drove Road, about half a mile further inland (Figs 47 and 48).

Seaside resorts wished to be associated with good health, but many suffered from very poor hygiene standards. This was due to people depositing waste into cesspools that seeped into water supplies or because they pumped sewage into the sea via outfalls that proved too short, leading to waste being washed back

Figure 47
The gasworks on Drove Road opened in 1856 and during the next 100 years the capacity increased to match the demand of the growing town. This detail from an RAF photograph, taken from the west, shows it as it was in 1958.
[RAF/58/2544/PSFO-P1 0017 25-AUG-1958]

onto the beach. Water was supplied from local pumps and wells. Outbreaks of cholera were eventually attributed to infected water supplies, and a number of seaside resorts suffered badly from epidemics of the disease. An editorial in the *Weston-super-Mare Gazette* in June 1849 shows the town's determination to head off any impact of the current cholera outbreak on its tourist trade; the article stated that Weston had been immune during a previous outbreak, and this would be likely to continue during the current one.

Figure 48
In 1912 the Gas Company completed a large
block of offices and stores in Burlington Street.
It is the last known work designed by Hans Price
and is now the town's museum.
[DP218736]

At Weston-super-Mare it may have been the prospect of the creation of the Montpelier Estate during the 1850s that galvanised the town into action. The 1851 Improvement and Market Act contained powers for the Improvement Commissioners to create a sewage system and charge people to connect to it, while another Act of Parliament in 1853 authorised the establishment of a company to supply the town with water. Water for the town's reservoir came from a spring at Ashcombe, where the waterworks was completed in 1854 (Fig 49). With the growth in the number of customers wanting piped water, a second reservoir was constructed on Worlebury Hill in 1866. The waterworks became the property of the Board of Health at a cost of £65,000 in 1878 and additional works subsequently took place, at a cost of £29,000.

Sewage treatment was a problem at seaside resorts from the outset. At Weston-super-Mare, a system, of sorts, was created in 1842–3, in which raw sewage was deposited into a rhyne draining through Uphill into the River Axe. Needless to say, the residents of Uphill were far from happy. Therefore, in 1852, depositing tanks were constructed and partial treatment was instituted before the sewage was released into the channel. In 1856 a new sewer was laid from Milton Road, along Ashcombe Road to the disinfecting works in Drove Road. However, the town still needed improved sewerage and therefore in 1865 the Board of Health employed Sir Joseph Bazalgette (1819–91), who had developed London's sewerage system, to design a new system for Weston. This included a new main sewer running from Orchard Street to the Drove Road sewage works and an outfall sewer from there to the mouth of the river Axe, where the partially treated sewage was discharged upon the ebb and swept into the sea round Brean Down.

Although seaside resorts had small populations compared to major cities, the annual influxes of holidaymakers, including trippers with no overnight accommodation, meant there was pressure to provide public conveniences. An issue to ponder is the impact that a lack of toilets had on the sight and smell of the seafront in the early days prior to purpose-built facilities being available (Fig 50).

Local government also had responsibility for safeguarding the growing town from the sea. A committee was set up on 3 December 1879 to begin dealing with legal formalities and a further committee was appointed in January 1880 to develop plans in association with T J Scoones, a consultant engineer

Figure 49
Not all of Weston-super-Mare was served by the town's reservoir; the Shrubbery Estate originally enjoyed its own water supply from a well and a Gothic-style water tower (pictured here) that Sophia Rooke had constructed. It was acquired by the Weston Waterworks in 1890 and survives today as a house. [DP218492]

Figure 50 (top)
A freestanding block of public toilets on the seafront
bears the date 1905. It is in an eclectic Edwardian
style, with plasterwork and timber framing providing
a hint of the Tudor in a building that is far from being
ashamed of its function. A seafront cafe now also
shares the site.
[DP218055]

Figure 51 (bottom)
The Seafront Improvement Scheme involved the
erection of gently sloping, stone-faced sea walls behind
which two miles of seafront promenade was created.
Wind-shelters and seats were provided at frequent
intervals. The work cost about £35,000 and required
1 million tons of stone.
[DP218026]

from Bristol. Local opposition to the removal of the sandhills, and general resistance to change, led to a public enquiry by the Local Government Board. It ruled in favour of the Seafront Improvement Scheme, which involved the creation of sea walls and a promenade. The foundation stone was laid on 15 March 1883 and the project was completed in August 1887 (Fig 51).

Caring for Victorian Weston

Seaside resorts came into existence to cater for the health needs, or equally the health whims, of wealthy Georgians. Doctors set up practices to treat influxes of patients, bathing machines populated the beaches of popular resorts and bathhouses were established for people who did not wish to bathe in the sea. Such health care was limited to the most prosperous, but by the late 18th century the seaside was already being recognised as an environment that would benefit the urban poor. The first institution to offer sea bathing treatments for London's poor who were suffering from scrofula was established at Margate in 1796, but it had only a limited impact in England, spawning similar institutions at Scarborough and Southport. In 1826 there was a proposal to establish the Somerset Sea-Bathing Infirmary, which was ready to accept five patients by the end of the year.[58] Whether or not any patients ever came to the infirmary is unknown, and there is apparently no further record of this institution or its location.

From the 1850s onwards the responsibility for providing burial places shifted from churches to local authorities, part of their increasing role in guaranteeing good public health. As a result of the Burial Act of 1855, Weston-super-Mare, like every town, had to provide a dedicated cemetery, independent of a churchyard. Churches prior to this date had attached burial grounds, but the new Christ Church of 1854–5 in the Montpelier Estate was designed without one, as was Holy Trinity in Atlantic Road in 1859–61. In 1856 a civic cemetery opened a short distance to the east of Christ Church, on land beside Ashcombe House. Covering around 7.5 acres (3ha), it was designed by Charles E Davis of Bath, who had won a competition in 1855 (Fig 52). It was extended in 1917, at which date it incorporated the gate lodge of Ashcombe House.

Figure 52
The civic cemetery originally had two Gothic-style
chapels, one for the Church of England and the other
for Nonconformists, now demolished. Like the cemetery,
the chapels were designed by Charles E Davis.
[DP218499]

Weston's hospital and dispensary was constructed in Alfred Street in 1864–5 by Hans Price, at a cost of about £950. It was enlarged in 1868 by the addition of the south wing, at a cost of £600, and in 1870 new wards for fever cases were added, at a cost of £300. The hospital was located at the edge of the rapidly growing working-class area to the north of the station and just to the south of the recently created Boulevard. Weston's small workhouse was built later on the edge of the hospital site, behind a terrace of houses on Alfred Street, and appears on the 1886 Ordnance Survey map. Additions were made to the hospital during the 1870s and 1880s, so that by 1891 there were 34 beds for patients. Further additions were made during the early 20th century, including a nurses' home in 1904 and a post-mortem room in 1910.

On the seafront, the West of England Sanatorium for Convalescents was established in 1868 to 'extend the benefit of the bracing air to the poorer classes', particularly for patients from hospitals in Western and Midland counties.[59] In 1871 the foundation stone of the present building was laid by the Earl of Carnarvon, in his capacity as Provincial Grand Master of Somerset, and by 1875 the sanatorium was providing 72 beds and had a Gothic chapel capable of seating a congregation of 150 (Fig 53). In 1890 £4,000 was spent on a seawater bathhouse on the seafront, which contained two large plunge baths and eight private baths. By 1911 the sanatorium had 156 beds and could care for approximately 3,000 patients each year.

As well as looking after the physical needs of Weston's population, the town also had responsibility for providing stimulation for the mind. Uplifting activities and educational institutions figure prominently in guidebooks. By 1871, museum specimens were exhibited in a building beside the Albert Memorial Hall, while a free library was established in Grove Park in the former residence of the Pigott family, which held about 3,000 volumes by 1894. A new Free Library and Museum was erected in 1899–1900 on the Boulevard to combine the two institutions as a belated celebration of Queen Victoria's Diamond Jubilee (Fig 54). The building cost about £3,500 and when the library opened in 1901, it contained 5,000 volumes.

Figure 53 (above)
Around £14,000 was spent on the original sanatorium, designed by Hans Price. Today the building has been converted into private apartments under the name of Royal Sands.
[DP218567]

Figure 54 (left)
The Renaissance-style library and museum contained a news room, reading room, librarian's room and the lending and reference libraries on the ground floor, while on the first floor two large rooms were used as the museum.
[DP218747]

Parks and gardens

Weston was amply provided with small, private gardens, which are often mentioned in complimentary terms in guidebooks, while new estate developments such as the Shrubbery had larger but still private gardens. Ellenborough Park is located between the seafront and Ellenborough Crescent and had villas to the north and south of it. The Crescent was built in 1855, and presumably the gardens were created at the same time or soon after (*see* Fig 26). Elaborate shrubberies are shown in an engraving of 1864 and in 1868 its 'pleasure grounds, shrubberies, walks, fountains &c ... [were] a most attractive addition to this already popular watering place'.[60] This was a garden for the residents, though the public could have looked on admiringly. Alexandra Parade Gardens, originally known as The Plantation, were created on the site of Weston's first railway station and the accompanying railway line, which closed in 1866. They are shown on the 1886 Ordnance Survey map with three longitudinal lines of trees and by the 1930s the site had elaborate gardens with trees and shrubs, and in 1935 a floral clock.

By the 1880s, the town was acquiring land for public parks, including the Prince Consort Gardens overlooking Birnbeck Pier. This land was unsuitable for substantial development and hence it was donated by the Pigott Estate. It had already been laid out as a private garden in 1862, much to the annoyance of excluded local people. It passed into public hands in 1882 and was rearranged in the mid-1880s. It had a conservatory with a series of circular rooms, one of which was used as an aviary, while another housed plants, with niches around the walls for busts (Fig 55).

The 16 acres (6.5ha) of land that became Clarence Park were donated to the town by Rebecca Davies in memory of her late husband, Henry Davies, in October 1882, an event commemorated by a brass plaque on one of the gateposts on the edge of the park (*see* Fig 27). However, the park did not open until 10 September 1889, its official opening having been postponed when Rebecca Davies died two days before the planned event. Spencer Tyler, chairman of the Town Commissioners, donated a fountain in her memory, which was turned on in September 1889. The park provided residents and holidaymakers with two public bowling greens and facilities used by the local hockey, tennis and archery clubs.

The local authority provided the Recreation Grounds adjoining the railway station, which opened on 12 September 1885 at a cost of £2,500. They provided a quarter-mile (400m) cinder track, a cricket pitch and a football field. There were two grandstands, one capable of holding 500 spectators, as well as a refreshment bar, dining and dressing rooms and toilets. The cinder track was for athletes and cyclists; a cycling club having already been founded in 1878, soon after the first safety bicycle had been patented.

The Grove was released by the Pigott Estate to the local authority on a perpetual rent in 1889 and opened as a public park on 20 June 1891. Grove Park had shelters and a bandstand in which regular 'high-class concerts' took place (Fig 56) and there were flower shows and open-air entertainments regularly during the summer.[61] Ashcombe Park was acquired by the Urban District Council from two farmers and formally opened on 19 June 1902. Covering 36 acres (14.6ha) in the east end of the town, far from the seafront, it provided residents with tennis courts and a bowling green.

Industry and technology

Industry in Victorian Weston

The first industrial activities in Weston-super-Mare were small-scale ones servicing the town's growth and the needs of its increasing number of inhabitants. These included smithies, sawmills, coal yards and carriage works in the working-class areas in and around Carlton Street and Oxford Street. Palmer Street, north of the railway station, has regular, large archways giving access through to yards behind the houses. However, perhaps the most visible sign of industrial activity in Weston-super-Mare was the Town Quarry on the hillside, which was in use by 1815 and continued in operation until 1953 (Fig 57). Further inland, Weston's largest quarry opened at Milton during the 1850s, and was taken over by Henry Butt in the mid-1880s.

Figure 57
The Town Quarry (pictured here) and another at Milton were the main sources of the local stone used in Weston's housing boom from the mid-19th century onwards. Builders also used stone imported from around Bath for dressings and fine detailing.
[DP218544]

As Weston's population grew, trade directories and guidebooks show an increasing number of tradesmen and services. The vast majority of these were small-scale businesses, but at Worle a brewery was founded in 1795. The company was put up for sale in 1865 and was purchased by the Weston-super-Mare Brewing and Malting Company, which was largely a creation of Henry Davies. The company was wound up in 1868, the year of Davies's death, and the brewery building stood empty until 1879, when it was converted into a laundry.

Weston-super-Mare also manufactured various types of aerated mineral waters from the 1850s onwards. In 1869 William M Forty acquired the Weston and West of England Soda Manufactory, which had small premises in Orchard Street. The company, renamed Ross and Co, moved to larger premises in Lower Bristol Road, beside what is now the YMCA building. This new building was originally erected as a roller-skating rink, a fad that soon passed, leaving a large, redundant building. Soft drinks were made by at least two other concerns: John Parrett and H T George produced them at the Westwick Brewery at Worle, established in 1863, and W G Carpenter had a business at the rear of 73 George Street from 1898 onwards.

During the 19th century, one industrial concern in Weston went from serving a predominantly local market to catering for substantial numbers of customers throughout the country. The Royal Pottery began life as two separate businesses. John Harvey owned a brickyard and kiln in the Locking Road area by 1836. In 1841 William Wilcox took over the Weston-super-Mare Brick and Tile Manufactory, as it was called, and worked it for the next six years. In about 1843 Samuel Serle set up an adjacent works, which was managed by Charles Phillips (1816–94). Not content with simply managing a brickyard, Phillips bought Wilcox's works next door in January 1847 and two or three years later he bought the other yard, amalgamating the two works for the first time. On an 1853 map the site is described as Phillips Pottery, Brick & Tile Manufactory, and is obviously an amalgamation of two businesses. Once Phillips owned his own yard, he began to experiment with products other than bricks and tiles, particularly flowerpots and garden ornaments, as well as statuary and fountains.

By 1851, when Phillips owned both potteries, he was employing 30 men and his pots received an honourable mention at the Great Exhibition. In 1854, despite accolades and what ostensibly seems to have been a thriving business, Philips was declared bankrupt and was forced to sell a number of properties to

clear his debts, including the original pottery (the western part of the works)
to Messrs Wilcox and Harvey. In March 1871 Charles Philips retired; the Royal
Pottery was sold to John Matthews (1824–92) and by 1874 it was producing
20,000 to 30,000 flowerpots every day (Fig 58). In 1885 Conway Gould Warne
(1863–1923) took over Wilcox's business and in spring 1888 Matthews retired
and sold the Royal Pottery to Warne, again unifying the businesses.

Figure 58
This view shows John Matthews's Royal Pottery,
suggesting it dates from the 1870s or 1880s.
[North Somerset Library Service]

During the 1890s housing development was coming ever closer to the pottery, restricting where new deposits of clay could be dug, and therefore a new site had to be found. Before 1883, William Wilcox had already set up a kiln and works to the south of Locking Road, close to the railway line. Warne decided to extend the New Pottery, which was renamed the Weston-super-Mare Pottery, Tile and Brick Co Ltd, and all production was transferred to this new site. The old potteries were demolished in 1897; the clay pits were filled gradually with the town's refuse and housing was built on the site.

In 1923 a large fire destroyed the main building of the New Pottery, sparing only one kiln but causing the loss of all the handmade wooden moulds for ornate designs dating from the previous century. Production was interrupted for several months, but despite this setback the 1920s proved to be a successful time for the business. However, with the coming of the Depression, the construction boom ended and the pottery shifted from predominantly brickmaking back to producing flowerpots, which was more profitable. Flowerpot production continued throughout World War II, but the arrival of the plastic flowerpot led to the final demise of the pottery, which went into voluntary liquidation in November 1961.

The Commercial Cable Company

The Commercial Cable Company was established in 1883 by John William Mackay (1831–1902), a mining magnate, and James Gordon Bennett (1841–1918), the owner of the *New York Herald*, to compete with the Western Union Atlantic service. In 1884 two cables were laid between Canada and Waterville (Co Kerry) in Ireland, from where one was linked to Le Havre in France and the other to Britain in June 1885, making landfall at Weston-super-Mare. Before the construction of a purpose-built facility, a pair of cottages was used as the cable office. An advertisement appeared in the *Weston Mercury* on 13 April 1889 seeking tenders for alterations to the 'Atlantic Cable Office' in Weston-super-Mare. The advertisement was signed by the local architect Sydney J Wilde and in May 1890 a feature in the *Western Daily Press* described the recently constructed building, which survives today in Richmond Street. This building was required to retransmit signals, which were weak after having crossed the Atlantic, and it was linked directly to London by landlines. The strategic significance of the cable office explains why it was guarded by troops during the wars and was a target for the Luftwaffe. In 1962 the office closed and is now in use as a bar/restaurant (Fig 59).

Figure 59
The left and right pairs of windows of the eastern half of the former Commercial Cable Company office (furthest from view in the main photograph) have roundels beneath them depicting the company logo, which was the route of the cable across the Atlantic. The central pair of windows has a roundel below with the initials of the Mackay Bennett Company. [DP218272, DP218273, DP218274]

Electricity and getting around Weston

Electricity did not come to Weston-super-Mare until May 1901, a decade after powers had first been granted for its provision. The reason for the delay seems to have been economic; the provision of electric lighting came about only when the Weston-super-Mare and District Electric Supply Company realised the possibility of running trams by day while lighting the streets by night, maximising their potential income. The company was established in 1899 and a Tram Order was obtained in 1900 to give it the necessary powers, including authorisation to raise capital of £80,000. A power station (designed by local architects Wilde & Fry) was constructed at Locking Road with direct access to the adjacent Great Western Railway line to allow for deliveries of coal. Initially the power station provided lighting for 134 customers, but by 1907 this figure had risen to 260. This is a very small number when compared to the fact that during the first year of operation, the trams carried 778,965 passengers. The route of the tramway was originally to be along Regent Street, with one line turning northwards towards Birnbeck Pier and the second heading southwards towards the sanatorium. When constructed, the route used was along Oxford Street instead. Work began in January 1902 and by April the first trial runs of trams were taking place (Fig 60).

Figure 60
The official opening of the tram service took place in May 1902. This interwar photograph shows Claremont Crescent in the background, with the sea to the left.
[North Somerset Library Service]

Even before Weston was creating its tram network, a scheme to link the town to Clevedon and Portishead, further north, by a light railway was taking shape. Despite their geographical proximity, there was no straightforward way of travelling between the three coastal towns. Therefore, in 1885 an Act of Parliament authorised the creation of a light railway, but work does not seem to have begun for several years due to the slow pace of acquiring land. By November 1889 only four miles of the route had been completed and after a tortuous, almost decade-long construction programme characterised by practical, financial and administrative setbacks and delays, the first recorded train between Weston and Clevedon ran on 18 August 1897. Portishead was connected a decade later, the first train travelling there on 7 August 1907.

The Weston, Clevedon and Portishead Light Railway had its Weston terminus at the junction of Milton Road and Ashcombe Road and the route headed eastwards through the growing town before turning northwards. The first part of the route still exists as a cycleway/walkway, the Colonel Stephens Way. The company obtained powers to extend its route to the Boulevard and tracks were laid along Gerard Road and the Boulevard in 1897. However, the Urban District Council objected because it claimed that the rails stood above the road surface and were therefore dangerous. The company refused to modify the arrangements and so the tracks were lifted and the scheme abandoned before any services had run.

From the outset, trams faced competition from buses, and opposition from taxi drivers. In 1934 the local bus operator, Burnell, was taken over by the Bristol Tramways Co and there were other bus services operated by the Great Western Railway. The Bristol Tramways Co began operating buses on the tram route within Weston during the summer and soon reached an agreement to close the town's tramway, purchasing it for £15,000, while paying the Urban District Council another £5,000 to lift the rails. The last tram ran in April 1937. Weston-super-Mare was the 102nd tramway system to close in Great Britain, and by 1962 Blackpool alone continued to operate a service. During their lifetime, Weston's trams carried more than 51 million passengers. The growing number of cars, improved bus services and a lack of people wishing to travel between the three towns led to the line to Clevedon and Portishead being closed on 18 May 1940.

The Victorian and Edwardian holiday in Weston-super-Mare

During the 18th century, a holiday to the seaside was normally restricted to a few people with the disposable wealth and free time to be able to enjoy staying away from home for weeks. Georgian seaside resorts catered for small numbers of affluent tourists, by providing small-scale sociable facilities and by making most of these accessible only by monthly or seasonal subscription rather than a single admission fee. By doing this, circulating libraries and assembly rooms could guarantee exclusivity; bathhouses were expensive and beyond the pocket of working people, but at theatres, anyone could potentially be admitted, though their experience and the company they kept would vary according to their ticket price. The vast majority of Georgian seaside tourists would stay in lodgings, taking rooms in a house where the landlord or landlady cooked the food the holidaymakers had purchased earlier in the day.

In contrast, by the end of the 19th century, well-developed Victorian resorts were catering for growing numbers of visitors coming by train and steamer. Where once dozens or hundreds of wealthy sea bathers stayed for weeks at a seaside resort, by 1900 thousands, and sometimes hundreds of thousands, of holidaymakers and day trippers flocked to beaches and bars, the latter activity attracting considerable comment from Victorian moralists. Some of the exclusive institutions that had entertained the wealthy elite continued, though often their seasonal customers moved to quieter resorts beyond the reach of the railways, and increasingly to resorts abroad. New and larger forms of entertainment venue were needed to cope with thousands of customers, and the advances in construction technology that had contributed to Britain's growing wealth were now applied to providing for its fun. Lodgings remained the main means of housing holidaymakers, but an activity once practised only by wealthy householders welcoming similarly affluent visitors spread to potentially any house with a room to let.

Respectable entertainment for respectable people

Weston-super-Mare broadly follows this story. However, the town's prosperity and success during the second half of the 19th century seems to have been more dependent on respectable, God-fearing residents, rather than boisterous trippers,

as the presence of a substantial YMCA demonstrates (Fig 61). This is clear
from guidebooks – at most resorts these books aim to inform and attract
visitors, while also providing useful information for local people. At Weston,
the guidebooks seem to be squarely aimed at respectable residents. There is
considerable emphasis on the clubs and societies that existed in the town,
including Conservative and Liberal clubs, Masonic lodges and similar venues
for Oddfellows, Foresters, Shepherds, Patriots, Good Templars and Sons of
Temperance. There were active musical and literary societies, and sporting
opportunities ranged from golf, bowls and cricket to fishing, archery, croquet
and even chances to go hunting.

The target audience for guidebooks included many people who had
retired to Weston. Censuses reveal a high number of people living in Weston
who are described as being of independent means, fundholders or annuitants,
and when combined with their ages, it suggests they were retirees. Therefore,
it is no surprise that from an early date publications seek to emphasise the
town's respectability and health-giving qualities, not only in the summer, but
also during the winter, a market first exploited by resorts on the south coast.
An 1850 directory noted:

> Weston is a favourite and well-frequented watering place, the fixed abode of
> many affluent families, a summer resort of almost numberless fashionable
> visitors, and the winter residence of scores of invalids and others in search
> of health, for whose accommodation, a variety of houses have been erected
> on charming sites; its hillsides are studded with temples of health and
> mansions of the rich; and its ocean-bounded valley is thickly covered with
> handsome habitations, in rows and detached, consisting partly of shops, but
> chiefly lodging houses close to the sea.[62]

As early as 1854 a guidebook described how the winter evenings were
enlivened by concerts, balls, lectures and exhibitions of a literary and scientific
order. By the early 20th century, guidebooks record how busy Weston was
during the winter, with visits from touring theatre companies, readings,
lectures and entertainments, ranging from dramatic recitals to conjuring tricks.

Where entertainments are discussed in guidebooks and directories, the
emphasis is often towards the more uplifting, the moralists' obsession with

Figure 61
Formed in Weston in October 1875, by 1887 the
YMCA had taken over Trafalgar House on Bristol
Road Lower. It contained a room for public meetings
and lectures, a reading room, a lecture room,
a study, a library with over 1,000 volumes and
accommodation for boarders in the house, as well
as a large gymnasium at the rear. The building
still functions as a YMCA centre.
[DP218743]

rational recreation being evident. An 1854 guidebook described the amusements available in Weston-super-Mare as 'generally of a rational and innocent kind'.[63] What is also clear is that two of the key entertainment institutions of the Georgian period continued to flourish in Victorian Weston, with guidebooks regularly listing and advertising circulating libraries and the assembly rooms. In the case of the latter, this was a new venture of 1858–9, replacing the old assembly rooms at the seaward end of Regent Street. A newspaper article in April 1859 announced the forthcoming opening of the assembly rooms. This would be marked by performances by 'several of the leading artistes of the day', including the celebrated Polish violinist and composer Henryk Wieniawski (1835–80). The article stated, 'Such a combination of talent will doubtless prove highly attractive, and the concerts being under distinguished patronage, there is little doubt there will be a large and fashionable attendance.'[64] The main hall at the new assembly rooms could hold 500 people, making it Weston's largest venue for over 20 years.

As the opening of the assembly rooms demonstrates, respectable music and entertainment were key elements of Victorian rational recreation. Moralists and guidebooks alike often frowned on the raucous behaviour and loud songs of minstrels and pierrots, and at some resorts they might be specifically banned from performing on the seafront and beach. At Weston, respectable musical fare was available in the parks, as well as in concert venues. An 1872 guidebook noted, 'During the Summer season, the attractions of the town are further enhanced by a splendid band, which plays at stated times at the Grove, Prince Consort Gardens, Ellenborough Park, and the Royal Hotel Field.'[65] Henry Mogg's band was founded in 1887 and went on to entertain Weston until 1929, winning the national band championship at the Crystal Palace, in London, in 1912. In 1920 H C Burgess's Orchestra was formed and soon became a permanent feature in the town, regularly performing at Rozel and the Winter Gardens until 1938.

Weston's piers

The character of the opening night festivities at the new assembly rooms demonstrates that this was not a facility aimed at large numbers of tourists, but a respectable venue for genteel Weston and its polite visitors. However, the town was already beginning to experience significant influxes of holidaymakers, and particularly day trippers in search of fun. Steamers had begun to call occasionally at Weston during the early 19th century; the *Duke of Argyll*, built at Port Glasgow in 1814, was the first to ply the Severn and regular packet services were in operation by 1821. The high tidal range severely restricted the development of steamer services and this is the reason that Weston undertook the construction of a pier in 1845. The only seaside piers constructed before this, designed for landing tourists and providing a pleasant promenade, were at Ryde on the Isle of Wight, Granton at Edinburgh, Brighton, Margate, Southend-on-Sea, Herne Bay and Gravesend.

Weston-super-Mare's first pier was the short-lived and never-completed suspension-bridge design on the site of the current Birnbeck Pier. Inspiration for the scheme came from two chain piers constructed a quarter of a century earlier – at Granton, near Edinburgh, and Brighton. A suspension-bridge form was an ambitious approach to pier design, an alternative to piled jetties, such as the pier at Ryde and the first timber jetty built at Margate during the 1820s. It was pioneered by the civil engineer and naval officer Captain Samuel Brown (1776–1852), who erected the Chain Pier at Granton in 1821 and another pier with a suspension structure at Brighton in 1823.

The Visitor's Companion in Rambling about Weston of 1847 has a frontispiece showing the design of Weston's proposed chain pier connecting Birnbeck Island to the mainland (Fig 62).[66] Work began on the vertical supports of the pier in 1847. However, a major storm later in the year swept away the first stonework of the uprights, leaving only foundations. There were no funds to continue work, the engineer James Dredge was declared bankrupt and the pier company was wound up.

Despite the failure of the pier project, steamers still landed passengers, when the tide was right, at a jetty on Knightstone Island, at Anchor Head and in the Axe Estuary. The first steamer to run an excursion was a tug called the *Sampson* in 1843 and various other excursions took place during the 1840s. To improve steamer services, an unsuccessful scheme was launched in 1854 to link the main railway line to Uphill, where a port would be equipped with suitable facilities. In 1861 Richard Jones, a fisherman, advocated the construction of a pier where later the Grand Pier would be constructed. At the same time as Jones was sketching out his design, there were more concrete moves to create a harbour at Brean Down. A company was incorporated with a capital of over £365,000 and

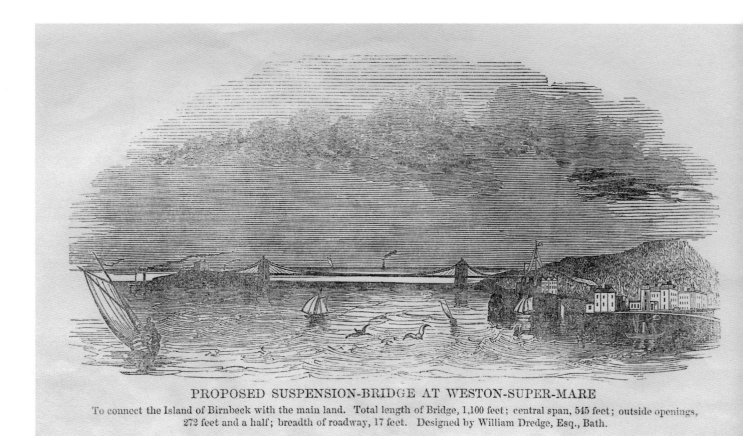

PROPOSED SUSPENSION-BRIDGE AT WESTON-SUPER-MARE

To connect the Island of Birnbeck with the main land. Total length of Bridge, 1,100 feet; central span, 545 feet; outside openings, 272 feet and a half; breadth of roadway, 17 feet. Designed by William Dredge, Esq., Bath.

Figure 62
Dredge's Pier was to be 335m long and carried on substantial stone piers. This view of 1847 lovingly records the elegant profile of the proposed pier, but shows only a single, small cuboidal block on Birnbeck Island, suggesting that the journey across was initially to be more important than the destination.
[North Somerset Library Service]

the foundation stone of the harbour was laid on 5 November 1864. Work continued until December 1872, when a violent storm destroyed the jetty; the scheme was revived in 1887, but came to nothing. Neither of the 1860s schemes bore fruit, but they seem to have been part of the discussions taking place in Weston-super-Mare about the desirability of providing a pier, which would culminate in the construction of Birnbeck Pier.

The Weston-super-Mare Pier Company, registered in January 1860, was largely a creation of the Smyth Pigott Estate, but also attracted investment from businessmen in the town and some interest from investors in south Wales.

The foundation stone of Birnbeck Pier was laid on 28 October 1864 and it was officially opened on 6 June 1867 (Fig 63). During the first three months of operation, 120,000 people passed through the turnstiles and receipts for this period totalled £5,000.

The designer was the renowned Victorian pier engineer Eugenius Birch (1818–84). His pier-building career began with the new jetty at Margate (1853–6), the first pier of the 14 he would design during a career that helped to define the essential characteristics of a pleasure pier. While Birnbeck Pier visually and structurally resembles other contemporary piers, it uniquely uses an island as part of its pier head.

The pier consisted of a 317m-long main structure between the mainland and Birnbeck Island, with originally a 12m-long timber jetty resting on iron piles, extending westwards. The jetty was dismantled in 1872 and replaced by

Figure 63
The components of Birnbeck Pier were erected by Messrs Toogood from parts prefabricated at their Isca Foundry, across the Severn in Newport in south Wales. The bridge section was completed by the end of 1866 and the pier officially opened in 1867.
[DP218350]

another one, 76m long, facing north. In 1882 a lifeboat was first stationed on the island, though a boathouse was not constructed for another eight years. The stone pavilion was built in 1884, the use of this material being made possible by the presence of the island, and it contained a concert hall and refreshment rooms. It was destroyed by fire on 26 December 1897, but was replaced by a new building by Price & Wooler that opened for business in July 1898. A low-water landing stage was added in 1898, but in September 1903 both jetties were badly damaged in the same storm that also damaged the seafront, breached Knightstone Causeway and destroyed all the bathing machines. The north jetty was rebuilt in steel and extended to 91m in length, but the low-water landing stage remained closed until 1910.

The large area and the stable footings provided by the island allowed substantial fairground rides to be erected by the early 20th century (Fig 64). The increasingly boisterous and commercial dimension of the island seems to have upset some local residents, who objected to the construction of a concrete

Figure 64
Among the attractions on Birnbeck Pier in the early 20th century were a water chute, a switchback railway, a shooting gallery, a helter-skelter, a merry-go-round and a flying machine. This consisted of a tall metal pylon from which hung gondola-shaped seats that swung out as the machine rotated. The stone building in the bottom right of this photograph was Birnbeck's first lifeboat boathouse, built in 1890; a newer lifeboat boathouse was built in 1902 (left).
[PC48002]

platform to increase its size. However, the extension was built on the south side of the pier, opening on 29 May 1909. It housed the theatre, a bio-scope (cinema) and a roller-skating rink.

These entertainments and amusements helped the pier to achieve a profit of over £3,000 during the summer of 1913. It also benefited from having a monopoly of steamer services landing passengers from around the Severn Estuary and especially from south Wales. The construction of the Grand Pier at the beginning of the 20th century had threatened this monopoly, but difficulties with navigation and currents prevented steamers ever successfully mooring alongside it, despite the building of a low-water-jetty extension.

The idea of a pier at the western end of Regent Street, where the Grand Pier is located, had been floated as early as 1861. In 1883 the idea was revived by the Weston-super-Mare Board of Health. It approved plans for a new promenade pier, over a mile in length, costing £70,000, as a central part of the scheme for a new seafront. Despite enthusiastic local meetings, no work took place. During the 1890s, this idea was revived and an Act of Parliament received its royal assent in 1893. However, there was no progress immediately and work finally began on 7 November 1903 to designs produced by Peter Munroe. By the summer of 1904 the contractors, Mayoh & Haley of London, had completed the pavilion and the first stage of the pier, and these opened on 11 June 1904 (Fig 65). Initially 329m long, a narrow, low-water landing stage was added in 1906, taking the pier to a total length of 786m, less than half the anticipated length of the original design. Only three steamers attempted to use the pier and once the approach channel had rapidly silted up, other pleasure-steamer captains refused to call there.

Without income from steamers, the pier had to focus on raising revenue from entertaining visitors. A 1910 guidebook described how it was famous for its high-class instrumental music and entertainments.[67] At the end of the pier there was a pavilion in which musical entertainments and vaudeville parties were staged for audiences of 2,000, and there were concert parties on the new stage behind the pavilion. A 1913 guidebook stated, 'The interior of the Pavilion is tastefully decorated in white and gold, and has a blue-tinted panelled ceiling.'[68] There was a bandstand in front of the pavilion and the pier also offered roller skating, confetti carnivals and many other seasonal attractions.

Gardens and Pier, Weston-super-Mare

Figure 65
The Grand Pier's original pavilion was destroyed by fire in 1930 and its replacement also succumbed to fire in 2008. This early 20th-century postcard also shows the seafront tram, a number of horse-drawn carriages and some early motor cars.
[PC08229]

Holiday attractions at Weston in the Victorian and Edwardian era

The first destination for holidaymakers and trippers arriving at Weston-super-Mare during the Victorian era was undoubtedly the beach. An 1854 guidebook recorded, 'The strand is well supplied with commodious and strongly-built bathing machines, which are kept extremely clean and neat.'[69] A bylaw of 1869 stipulated that male and female bathers should be kept 200 yards (183m) apart and that bathers had to use machines if they were entering the sea within a quarter of a mile (402m) of a dwelling house. The Revd Francis Kilvert, who stayed at Princes Buildings in 1872, reluctantly used a bathing machine, recording the event in his diary:

Wednesday, 4 September

Bathing in the morning before breakfast from a machine. Many people were openly stripping on the sands a little further on and running down into the sea, and I would have done the same but I had brought down no towels of my own.[70]

The following day he had obviously remembered his towel and bathed in exactly the way he liked – naked:

Thursday, 5 September

I was out early before breakfast this morning bathing from the sands. There was a delicious feeling of freedom in stripping in the open air and running down naked to the sea, where the waves were curling white with foam and the red morning sunshine glowing upon the naked limbs of the bathers.[71]

Men had bathed in the nude since the early 18th century, but Kilvert's diary reveals that he was probably one of the last to indulge in what was increasingly felt to be a scandalous practice, permitted only at the fringes of beaches and early in the day.

By the early 20th century, there had been a relaxation in the rules regarding bathing and bathing machines at Weston, and at seaside resorts in general. Bathing without machines was permitted before 9am and after 8pm on any part of the sands south of Severn Road and mixed bathing was allowed on one part of the foreshore. As well as bathing machines, tents were also available on the sands opposite the Grand Atlantic Hotel.

Increasingly, beaches were becoming 'the children's Paradise'. A 1901 guidebook described the fun children could enjoy on Weston-super-Mare's sands:

There they are, these bright-eyed, cheek-tanned, bare-legged little ones, fairly revelling, it seems, in this sense of security. Scores of them are exercising their ingenuity in building castles of sand, with wondrous ramparts and dark mysterious tunnels. And the donkey rides! Surely nowhere else does this fascinating form of childish amusement reach so nearly to perfection as it does at Weston, due, of course, largely to the fact that the incoming tide is not to be reckoned with to any serious extent.[72]

Away from the beach, the Knightstone Baths were still an important facility for residents and tourists. The baths were sold, or planned to be sold, in 1850, and were sold in 1860 and then again in 1880. On this occasion, they were sold to Mr Griffiths, who enlarged the open-air pool and built a covered pool for women on its north side. In 1891 Knightstone Island was bought by a company that intended to develop the commercial use of the wharf; 20,000 tons of coal was imported from south Wales here each year during the late 1880s and limestone was taken away. The only alteration to the baths at this date was an extension of 4.5m to the ladies' pool.

In 1894 Arthur's Tower and the other lodging houses on Knightstone Island were demolished and, soon after, the newly formed Weston Urban District Council decided to purchase the island for £13,482. Part of the island was extended using girders placed over an earlier swimming pool, thus providing more space for a large pavilion. On 13 May 1902 the new swimming pool and pavilion/opera house opened (Fig 66). The swimming baths cost £9,800 and the main pool had a gallery for 400 spectators. There was also a seawater swimming bath for ladies, an open seawater swimming bath and a number of slipper baths. The nearby pavilion and opera house, which cost around £20,000 to build, had a concert hall with a gallery around it, except at the stage end. It was capable of seating 2,000 people.

In 1881 the Weston-super-Mare Summer and Winter Gardens Co Ltd was established to create tennis courts and a pleasant garden with a large hall in it. The Victoria Hall, designed by Price & Wooler, opened on 19 December 1884 to the north of the Boulevard, between Victoria Quadrant and Albert Quadrant. The hall could accommodate 1,000 people and was attached to the Summer and Winter Gardens, which were entered from a porch reminiscent of a triumphal arch. By 1910 its proprietor, Michael William Shanly, had altered it so that he

Figure 66
This 1932 Aerofilms photograph, taken from the south-west, shows Knightstone Island, with the Georgian bathhouse on the western side, the swimming baths behind it and the Pavilion to the right. This photograph was taken soon after the Marine Lake was created in the late 1920s (see also Figs 71 and 94). [EPW039937]

could provide his customers with three daily roller-skating sessions on the Victoria Hall's 'perfect floor' and two cinematograph shows during the evening in another room.[73] The Victoria Hall later became a Palace of Varieties, then a theatre and finally the Tivoli Cinema in 1928.

Shanly was offering 'cinematographic entertainment' nightly at the Victoria Hall by 1910. During the following year some films were shown in the Knightstone Pavilion and in the same year Weston acquired its first purpose-built cinema, the Electric Cinema, on part of the site of the future Odeon Cinema. The Regent Cinema (later the Gaumont) in Regent Street followed, opening on 22 March 1913, and the Central Cinema opened in Oxford Street in 1921.

Staying in Victorian Weston

The first Victorian visitors to seaside resorts, like their Georgian predecessors, might stay at a simple hotel or a handful of inns, but this was usually just until they had secured lodgings. They took rooms, a floor of a house or even an entire house, either by prior arrangement or taking their chances on arrival at a resort. It is clear from guidebooks, censuses and diaries that any house might offer lodgings and any prospective customer might recognise an available room by a notice posted in a window or by word of mouth. Settled in their lodgings, guests would usually purchase their own food, which would be cooked by their host, but during the 19th century some landlords went further, becoming boarding houses which provided meals.

Early visitors would have stayed in any house that was available, not one constructed with the comfort of visitors in mind. However, by the early 19th century, the presence of tourists, and, perhaps more importantly, their return each year, led local people to build more comfortable and more substantial houses, the additional expense being affordable because of income that would be raised from lodgers. This was not cheap holidaymaking; it was wealthy middle-class people staying at the seaside. In 1851 the seven houses comprising Victoria Buildings on Knightstone Road were home to people of means, but also a builder and two lodging-house keepers. The adjacent Princes Buildings, of a similar date, had become dominated by lodging-house keepers in 1851, six of the seven houses providing accommodation for visitors. In the 1851 Census, Royal Crescent already had four houses providing lodgings; alongside Oriel Terrace, it was the most prestigious new development in Weston-super-Mare. Therefore, the presence of a retired major and a clergyman, alongside houses providing lodgings, suggests the status of the customers being catered for. Wealthy visitors would naturally gravitate towards these larger houses on or near the seafront and on the slope of the hill in search of rooms; less affluent visitors would leave the station and head into the working-class areas to the north and west.

Although the vast majority of people stayed in lodgings, other options were inns and small hotels, including temperance hotels, which catered for short-term stays, new arrivals and for people who preferred that type of accommodation (Fig 67). The largest hotel in Weston for much of the 19th century was the Royal Hotel (*see* p 10-11), constructed at the beginning of the 19th century and

Figure 67
Weston had a number of temperance houses and hotels; in 1905 the Shaftesbury Hotel was a 'high-class temperance' establishment, located in the angled, corner block in the centre of Hans Price's Magdala Buildings of 1870. Discolorations on the upper parts of the facade show where signs were located.
[DP218650]

enlarged to almost its current size in 1849. However, by the 1860s major seaside resorts were beginning to build hotels on a much larger scale and with more sophisticated facilities. The largest seaside hotels at this date were Brighton's Grand Hotel, which opened in 1864, and the Grand Hotel at Scarborough. It opened in 1867 and contained 300 bedrooms, reputedly making it Europe's largest hotel at that date. To rival these hotels, a prospectus was issued in 1886 by the Grand Hotel, Weston-super-Mare Ltd, with the intention of erecting a first-class hotel on the Grand Parade. However, instead of a new building, Weston-super-Mare was graced with the Grand Atlantic Hotel, which opened on 13 July 1889, an enlargement and adaptation of the College of 1859 (Fig 68; see p 62). The architect, John S Whittington of Manchester, 'introduced every conceivable improvement and modern appliance' into the building.[74] The newspaper article celebrating its opening also described the accommodation. The ground floor had a dining room, a reception room, a sitting room, a billiard room with two full-size tables, a smoking room and other apartments. The best bedrooms and sitting rooms were on the first floor and on every landing there were sets of toilets and bathrooms for ladies and gentlemen. An elevator ran from the basement to the top of the hotel.

Figure 68
Examination of the Grand Atlantic Hotel's facade reveals that the original elevation of the College survives, but the building has been extended on either side by wings with polygonal, corner turrets. It has also been raised to four storeys, with an attic throughout (see Fig 45).
[DP218759]

At the start of the 20th century, Weston-super-Mare boasted two piers, a major hotel, ample lodging houses, modern services and a rapidly growing population. When peace returned in 1918 after World War I, the town was well placed to welcome back tourists, though it was quick to recognise it would need further investment if it were to prosper in the 20th century.

Weston-super-Mare in the 20th century

4 Interwar Weston – improving the tourist facilities

Weston is one of the most up-to-date and enterprising watering places in the kingdom, and is well provided with handsome and commodious hotels, first-class boarding establishments, and innumerable lodging houses, so that the requirements of all classes are readily met.

The Borough Guide to Weston-super-Mare and its Neighbourhood, 1924[75]

Immediately after World War I, there was an air of business-as-usual in Weston-super-Mare. Guidebooks, such as the one quoted above, reveal the same range of holidaymaking activities and facilities as in 1914. Before the war, the number of excursionists each bank holiday in Weston had peaked at around 38,000, but in 1921 the August bank holiday crowds totalled 51,000 and reached 78,000 in 1937. In 1919 most visitors came by train, but by the 1930s as many people were arriving by car; this trend is evident in contemporary photographs, with the seafront becoming the car park that is so familiar today.

Standing still was not an option for a successful seaside resort; the growing number of tourists (people with modest but increasing disposable incomes) wanted more entertainment and better facilities. The interwar years therefore saw Weston Urban District Council taking a more interventionist role in the provision of facilities for holidaymakers, adopting a policy similar to high-spending resorts such as Blackpool and Hastings.

In 1922 the Urban District Council bought Rogers's Field, the still undeveloped plot between the High Street and the seafront, beside the Royal Hotel. This field had been suggested as the site for the Summer and Winter Gardens in 1881 (*see* p 91), but instead this facility had been created further inland beside the Boulevard. Quarry owner and developer Henry Butt (*see* p 106) had a long-drawn-out lawsuit with the council concerning the damage to the town's roads caused by his heavy lorries. He lost, but to show there were no hard feelings, he offered in 1925 to meet the cost of acquiring the field, as well as the arbitration proceedings. The council planned seafront Winter Gardens for the site: the Italian Gardens were the first part of the project to be

This 1928 Aerofilms photograph shows the busy seafront beside the Grand Pier, with trams, cars and horse-drawn carriages. There are also a couple of small charabancs parked on the seafront. [EPW023970]

completed, comprising the putting green, rose garden, lily pond and Alpine garden and opening to the public in August 1925 (Fig 69). On 14 July 1927 the pavilion, with its large ballroom, was officially opened by Sir Ernest Palmer, deputy chairman of the Great Western Railway (Fig 70).

Figure 69
This postcard shows the section of the gardens behind the Winter Gardens pavilion, probably soon after it opened in 1927. It also shows the tennis courts that were part of the scheme.
[PC09135]

Figure 70
Designed by T H Mawson with the borough engineer Harold Brown, the Winter Gardens pavilion provided the town with a larger ballroom and became home to H C Burgess's Orchestra. This modern, long-time-exposure image has the lights of cars streaking along the seafront road in front of it.
[DP218335]

A key concern of the local authority at Weston during the interwar years was to cater for the growing number of visitors who wished to swim and play in the sea, something that could be problematic at low tide. A scheme had been mooted as early as 1871 to enclose Glentworth Bay to allow bathers easy access to a body of seawater regardless of the tide. The idea was revived during the 1880s, and in 1888 the architect John S Whittington proposed creating a huge marine lake stretching from between Ellenborough and Clarence parks. In 1895 the newly created Urban District Council decided to support a proposal that envisaged creating a barrage from Knightstone Island to Black Rock at Uphill, an eye-watering distance of nearly 2 miles. By the 1920s a more realistic scheme had taken shape and by 1929 a barrage had been constructed between Knightstone Island and the shoreline near the southern end of Claremont Crescent, a more manageable distance of 270m (Fig 71).

Figure 71
The Marine Lake, photographed here from the north-east, was originally equipped with a diving stage, rafts, rubber boats, water chutes, children's paddle boats and hundreds of bathing tents and dressing enclosures. It was an instant success, being used by more than a quarter of a million people during 1929 (see also Figs 66 and 94).
[NMR 33066/008]

Weston Urban District Council also decided to construct an open-air bathing pool further south (Fig 72). At the opening ceremony in July 1937, a message from the government was read out: 'Any money which may have been expended upon [the pool] will come back a hundredfold ... not necessarily in cash, but in health, which is better than wealth.'[76] The entrance to the bathing pool on the seafront is a two-storey pavilion flanked by single-storey wings containing changing rooms and roof terraces (*see* Fig 98). Designed by the office of the borough engineer, Harold Brown, the architecture is an essay in stripped-down civic classicism and is in striking contrast to the elegant modernism of the

Figure 72
In its opening year the open-air bathing pool attracted 109,000 bathers and 156,000 spectators. This Aerofilms photograph of 1949, taken from the north-east, also shows the large number of parked cars along the seafront and on the beach, reflecting the way that most people now came to Weston. [EAW025157]

diving platform at the seaward end of the pool (Fig 73). It was described from the outset as 'the finest diving platform in Europe' and immediately became a symbol of the town, frequently featuring in posters produced by railway companies. It was built by Messrs George Pollard of Taunton, with reinforced concrete steelwork provided by Messrs Coignet of London. The contribution of Harold Brown to this part of the project is uncertain. By the 1970s, with the number of tourists declining, the bathing pool was becoming less popular and in February 1982 the diving stage was demolished. During the following year the bathing pool underwent a £1 million transformation and reopened as the

Figure 73
The diving platform at the open-air bathing pool consisted of two parallel reinforced concrete arches, 8m high, faced with a band of coloured tiles from which seven boards at 3m, 5m, 7m and 10m were cantilevered. This photograph was taken to mark its completion in 1937.
[BB81/08493]

Tropicana, a water park featuring slides, a fibreglass elephant and a giant pineapple. It closed in 2000 and the site is currently used as an events space.

As well as intervention by the Urban District Council, there was also some notable investment by the private sector. In January 1930 a fire destroyed the Grand Pier's pavilion and construction of a new building began in the autumn of 1932, funded by the pier's owners. The pier head was enlarged and strengthened to support the larger structure, designed by John Darby. The new pavilion opened in 1933 and a cafe and ballroom were added in 1935.

With growing numbers of tourists arriving each year, new facilities had to be larger than before and were therefore normally beyond the economic capacity of investors from the immediate locality. This explains why the intervention of local government was so important, and it is also the background to the creation of the Odeon Cinema in 1934–5, on the corner of Walliscote Road and Regent Street. The cinema opened on 25 May 1935, replacing the smaller Electric Premier Cinema on this prominent corner site beside the Goods Station (Fig 74). The Odeon was designed in 1934 by the Nottingham architect T Cecil Howitt (1889–1968; Fig 75) and was constructed by C Bryant & Son Ltd of Birmingham.

Figure 74 (left)
The Odeon Cinema originally had 1,174 seats in the stalls and 633 in the balcony. In 1973 it was divided into three screens and by 2001 the fourth screen had been created. This photograph was taken on its opening day in 1935.
[BB87/02803]

Figure 75 (opposite)
In addition to Weston's cinema (pictured here), T Cecil Howitt was responsible for designing four other Odeon cinemas: Warley, near Birmingham (1934); Clacton (1936, now demolished); Bridgwater (1936); and Bristol (1938). All of his Odeon cinemas featured a square tower with a projecting flat slab roof supported by squat, cylindrical columns.
[BB87/02801]

Living in Weston between the wars

The years between the two world wars saw local government actively intervening in the tourism industry more comprehensively than before. The same was true in the housing market, in response both to greater national government involvement, with consequent increased available funding, and to cater for the town's growing population. Weston's population continued to grow from 23,235 in 1911 to 31,653 in 1921, but in the 1920s there was a drop in population, against the national trend. This had recovered by 1951, when 40,165 people were living in Weston.

In general, interwar and post-war housing in Weston was influenced more by national trends than was the case with the town's Victorian and Edwardian housing, which managed to achieve a local distinctiveness. This was in part due to the emergence of council housing, and the use of prefabricated construction techniques, as well as changes of taste and the growth of national firms of speculative builders who propagated houses designed in 'stockbroker's Tudor'.

In Weston-super-Mare, as elsewhere, there was a housing shortage after World War I, caused by the slowing of any building activity before the war and then its total cessation for the duration. The 1919 Housing Act, also known as the Addison Act, introduced for the first time a government subsidy in order to prompt the construction of new council housing. In 1937 the new Borough Council claimed proudly that its predecessor had built the 'first houses in the country' under the Act at Milton Green (Fig 76), though similar claims were made by other local authorities across the country.[77] The houses at Milton Green are a group of 13 semi-detached homes around an elongated 'square', with further semis and double-length terraces along Milton Road to the north. They are instantly recognisable by the broad gables, either at the end bays or in the centre bay of each house.

Other public housing schemes were started during the late 1920s, for example around Osborne Road, off Locking Road, a site that had been acquired in 1928. In 1929 the Urban District Council started work on extending the Bournville Estate, originally a speculative development of around 1904. Stradling Avenue was one of the first roads built by the local authority and by 1931 more than 40 semi-detached houses and one terrace of three houses had been built there. By the time war broke out again, the estate had reached as far

Figure 76
The public housing at Milton Green was built shortly after the Housing Act of 1919 and is one of the earliest post-war schemes in the country.
[DP218579]

as Selworthy Road. Roads continued to be laid out during and after World War II, such as Coniston Crescent and the octagon formed by Scott Road, Byron Road, Shelley Road and Coleridge Road. The first houses to be built there were prefabricated, of the type known at the time as 'emergency factory made' houses, which are visible on aerial photos of 1948. Permanent houses were not built there until the 1950s. Similarly, the first shops on the estate were also prefabricated structures, which were replaced between 1953 and 1960 by two shopping parades at the crossing of Lonsdale Avenue and Baildon Road.

While the council took an active role in providing public housing during the interwar years, large numbers of private houses continued to be built, notably in Milton and Ashcombe, where the site of the historic Manor Farm was being redeveloped. These were generally of a standard interwar design. More unusual are the Art Deco houses in Neva Road and Station Road, which local architects Leete & Darby designed in 1934 (Fig 77). This group comprises eight flat-roofed semis with integral garages, two detached houses and two bungalows.

Figure 77
This modern photograph shows some of the Art Deco houses in Station Road, built in around 1934 to designs by Leete & Darby.
[DP218280]

The growing town also needed some new facilities. The hospital was enlarged during the late 1920s as a result of a public collection that raised £50,000. Two of Weston's most prominent citizens appear to have led the way and it is therefore fitting that on 11 November 1926 Henry Butt and Ernest Baker (*see* p 5) both laid commemorative stones and that the foundation stone was laid by the Venerable Walter Farrer, Archdeacon of Wells. The new general hospital building, dedicated to Queen Alexandra, was opened on 6 July 1928 by the Duke and Duchess of York. The hospital closed in 1986, when a new one opened at Uphill.

A new magistrates' court and police station (*see* Fig 95) opened in 1934, designed by the county architect, Major A J Toomer. Located on the corner of Walliscote Road and Station Road, diagonally opposite the Town Hall, it is faced in stone and is two storeys high and seven bays wide. The large entrance on Station Road was the Justices' Entrance, according to a sign, while there were two doorways in the Walliscote Road elevation, the right-hand doorway being the public entrance and the second doorway for official court users. The building contained three courtrooms on the first floor. In 1970 the police moved to a new purpose-built police station to the rear of the 1934 building, following the demolition of four police houses the year before.

Henry Butt and the 'mansions'

While the council led the way in the provision of new housing, one man was at the forefront of transforming a significant part of the town's existing housing stock, by subdividing large houses into flats. Robert Henry Coate Butt (1861–1944), known as Henry, is best remembered as Weston's first mayor, who received the town's charter from the Lord Lieutenant in 1937, and as a major quarry owner (Fig 78). Aged 18, he came to Weston to take over the management of the local branch of the Somerset Trading Company, where he had started two years earlier as an office sweeper, and successfully increased their turnover, notably by providing cheaper haulage with his own horses and carts. He developed numerous commercial interests, from quarries and limekilns to property speculation. By the time he left the Somerset Trading Company in 1891, he is said to have owned around 12 different businesses, including Henry Butt Ltd Co, a coal, timber and general merchant's business. Butt also held several public offices, and was, for example, a county councillor for 25 years, a

Figure 78
Henry Butt, a quarry owner and developer, in a portrait taken during his time as 'charter mayor' for the celebration of the town's new status as Borough Council. [Borough of Weston-super-Mare Charter Souvenir 1937, 15]

HENRY BUTT, J.P. (Charter Mayor)

hospital governor for 20 years, chairman of the local gas company and a justice of the peace. When he died in 1944, he left a fortune of £84,866, which is the equivalent of over £3 million today.

Butt's property speculation started shortly after he arrived in Weston. He bought seven houses at an auction, improved them and leased them on a ground rent, making over £1,000 in seven months. However, his most significant architectural legacy was the extension and conversion of numerous large Victorian houses into flats (Fig 79). In 1914, shortly after the war had started, Butt bought 100 houses within six weeks and started to convert them into flats, a process of acquisition and conversion that continued throughout the interwar

Figure 79
This pair in Victoria Quadrant was among many Victorian houses acquired by Henry Butt and converted into flats during the interwar period. It is now known as Bouverie Mansions (right-hand side) and Hibernia Mansions (left-hand side).
[DP218645]

period. In 1938 he described himself as the 'owner of 300 flats'.[78] He later claimed that for nine years he completed a flat conversion every fourteen days. The conversions were more than mere subdivisions of large houses: generally, a large side or rear extension was built, in addition to providing new entrance arrangements by means of external stairs or bridges over a front area. The new extensions were skilfully executed and are frequently indistinguishable from the original fabric. He renamed them 'mansions' and had their new names carved over or near the entrances; such signs can be found throughout the town, with a particular concentration around Atlantic Road. They were generously sized flats and Butt may have overestimated the demand for such large flats, as from 1933 a second wave of conversions further subdivided them.

Interwar churches and schools

Weston's growing population between the wars needed new places of worship and schools. Several new churches were built, some of which replaced temporary premises of the pre-war years, while others served new and growing neighbourhoods and communities. There was a particular concentration of new churches in Milton, where a large proportion of interwar houses were built.

In 1928 the construction of a Roman Catholic church dedicated to Corpus Christi started in Ellenborough Park South and it opened a year later (Fig 80). It was designed by John Bevan of Bristol (1867–1950). The overall cost was £16,000, a surprisingly large sum for an interwar church, which is mainly due to its ornate Byzantine style, carvings and stained glass. Another new Catholic church, Our Lady of Lourdes, was built in Milton in 1938, with a much smaller budget of about £4,000. Instead of a richly decorated historicist style, the architects Roberts & Willman of Taunton used a free Gothic style, combined with reinforced concrete vaulting.

The Methodists also built two new places of worship during the period. In 1930 a new church by architects Ball & Pope was built at Milton Hill, which was restored in 1951 after war damage. Another, much grander church was built as a result of the fire in 1935 that destroyed the Victoria Methodist Church in Station Road (Fig 81). The new building of 1935–6 is in a simplified Gothic style using Pennant stone with Ham stone dressings, an approximation of the traditional

Figure 80
Corpus Christi Roman Catholic Church of 1928–9 has an elegant ashlar exterior and a fine Byzantine-inspired brick interior. [DP218753]

Figure 81
The Victoria Methodist Church of 1935–6 was built
after a fire destroyed the Victorian predecessor church.
It was designed by Fry, Paterson & Jones.
[DP218734]

building materials of Weston. The new church was deliberately placed on a
different orientation to its predecessor to make full use of the site, with the
chancel being orientated to the east instead of the south.

In 1929–30 the Baptists built a Gothic church by Fry, Paterson & Jones
in front of the dual-purpose hall in Walliscote Road, which had previously
been used as a church. The Baptists also built a new church in Baytree Road,
Milton, designed by Ball & Pope (since replaced). In 1925 the Congregationalists
celebrated their centenary in Weston with the opening of a Gothic church
by Fry, Paterson & Jones in Moorland Road.

After slowing down before 1914, Somerset County Council's school building
programme started again during the interwar years, when Weston's long-
planned secondary school was finally realised. In 1922 the County Grammar
School for boys and girls was established in temporary buildings in Nithsdale

Road but was replaced 13 years later by a large, new building designed by the county architect, Major A J Toomer, in Broadoak Road, Uphill. The building had a double courtyard plan and a central tower in the fashionable stripped classical style. It was demolished in 1999 when a new building opened on the eastern part of the site, now renamed Broadoak School.

The council's Bournville Estate was initially served by a joint infant and junior school, which opened on 17 February 1941. This became the infant school when a separate junior school opened in 1948. Both buildings, designed by the county council's architects' department, have been replaced by modern buildings.

Flight

The industries at work in Weston before World War I broadly continued during the interwar years, but the town also became the centre for an entirely new industrial activity. Some seaside resorts were quick to embrace the new technology of flying; Blackpool tried to organise the country's first aviation week in October 1909, but Doncaster hastily arranged an event during the preceding week to steal its thunder. Blackpool provided Britain's first scheduled daily air service in 1919 and developed one of the earliest municipal aerodromes in 1929.

Weston-super-Mare had a similarly pioneering spirit. *Flight* magazine recorded that, on 1 September 1911, 'during his visit to Weston-super-Mare, Mr C B Hucks decided to pay a visit by aeroplane to his one-time home at Cardiff, in what was the first double journey across the Bristol Channel in an aeroplane'.[79] Hucks is often claimed to be the first aviator to land at Weston, but a month earlier Samuel Cody was forced to land on the beach while flying between Bristol and Exeter during the Circuit of Britain Air Race.

Weston's airport had its first commercial landing on 31 May 1936 and it was officially opened by the Deputy Lord Mayor of Cardiff, who flew over to perform the ceremony on 25 June 1936. Work had only started on the airport in February of that year, under the watchful eye of Harold Brown, but by August the terminal and administrative building was nearly complete and nearby a large aircraft hangar was constructed (Fig 82). Since the airport had begun operating nine weeks earlier, Western Airways had already transported 8,000 passengers and the company was running an hourly service between Bristol and Cardiff,

and a new twice-daily service between Birmingham and Weston. Analysis of passenger numbers led *Flight* magazine to conclude, 'Holiday-makers will use the air while business people still view it with misgiving.'[80] As well as scheduled services to a growing number of destinations, pleasure flights took holidaymakers for trips over Weston and around the bay, and adverts for these trips can be found in guidebooks, particularly after World War II. During the war, the Air Ministry took over the airfield and in 1940 closed down the service between Weston and Cardiff.

Figure 82
This Aerofilms photograph of Weston-super-Mare's airport was taken in 1939, from the north-west. By this date, the small terminal building in the corner of the field was accompanied by two hangars. [EPW062080]

For a few short years at the end of the 1930s, Weston was looking to the future, hoping that aircraft would bring affluent holidaymakers to the town. However, like Blackpool, it would suffer during the post-war period because aircraft took a significant part of its traditional market elsewhere. Aircraft also had another impact on the town's future, the impact of air raids during World War II contributing to transforming the townscape of central Weston during the post-war years.

Weston-super-Mare at war

The nature of warfare during World War I meant that direct conflict was distant from Weston-super-Mare, which lay beyond the reach of Zeppelins and later Gotha bombers. And as there was a fixed front line for most of the war, there was no direct threat to the fabric of the town. However, the impact of the war would have been noticed and felt, with soldiers billeted in the town to guard strategic points, such as the piers and the Commercial Cable Company building in Richmond Street, but also to receive training and to convalesce after injury. Rogers's Field, later the site of the Winter Gardens, was used for drill until 1917, when it was turned over to allotments. There were also refugees in Weston; as early as October 1914 there were requests in the local press to house 100 displaced Belgian civilians for six months and there is a memorial in the town's cemetery to five refugees who died there, including a one-year-old child. While World War I may not have come directly to Weston-super-Mare, the town lost many of its sons and in 1922 the war memorial was unveiled in Grove Park.

World War II was a very different affair. Britain faced a serious invasion threat and this time the enemy was just across the Channel, with aircraft that could hit every part of the country. However, Weston was felt to be a relatively safe place, and therefore hosted evacuated women and children. Large, vacant houses were requisitioned by the armed forces and the general hospital was emptied to make way for expected military casualties. By 1940 most seaside piers had been breached to prevent enemy forces from landing troops, but as Weston was located on England's west coast, it was felt that a few troops could guard the Grand Pier, while Birnbeck Pier became HMS Birnbeck, a naval weaponry research establishment.

Sporadic, small-scale air raids took place from mid-1940 onwards, with the first bombs landing on Weston's beach on 14 August 1940. The first major air raid took place on 4 January 1941, when in the space of nine hours 3,000 incendiaries and 30 high-explosive bombs led to the deaths of 34 people, with a further 85 being injured. A second, larger and more sustained attack occurred on two successive nights on 28 and 29 June 1942, during which the town was hit by 100 high-explosive bombs and 10,000 incendiaries, resulting in the loss of 102 lives, with a further 400 people being injured. The victims were buried in their own plot within Milton Road Cemetery.

Among the sites destroyed during the war were the Tivoli Cinema, the Boulevard Congregational Chapel, Grove Park Pavilion and Lance and Lance's department store on the corner of Waterloo Street and High Street. There was also damage in Oxford Street, Orchard Street, Wadham Street, Prospect Place and along Union Street, as well as in further-out residential areas. St Paul's Church was gutted by fire (Fig 83), but restored after the war, and a number of prominent buildings and sites were damaged, including the open-air pool, Knightstone Baths and the public library. If the Cable Office, HMS Birnbeck, the railway line, the airport, RAF Locking and Weston's military-industrial production plants were the main targets, the Luftwaffe was unsuccessful.

Weston-super-Mare 1945–2000

Post-war master planning

The two decades after the end of World War II were dominated by discussions about two idealistic, almost utopian schemes that would have transformed Weston-super-Mare. After the war, Weston-super-Mare Borough Council invited Sir (Bertram) Clough Williams-Ellis (1883–1978) and the Hon Lionel Gordon Baliol Brett, later fourth Viscount Esher (1913–2004), to develop a plan for the future of the town. Williams-Ellis is most famous for the creation of the romantic holiday village of Portmeirion, in north Wales, which was begun in 1925, but due to his wife's close connection with the Attlee government, he became involved with finding solutions to the problems of post-war planning and reconstruction. This involved working on ideas for new towns, created as a result of the New Towns Act 1946, and led to him being the chairman of the

Figure 83
This photograph shows St Paul's Church after it was hit during an air raid on 4 January 1941.
[North Somerset Library Service]

Stevenage New Town Development Corporation for a short time. Williams-Ellis was briefly in partnership with Brett, and they were involved with developing a town plan for Littlehampton, in West Sussex, as well as Weston-super-Mare. Brett also worked on plans for Redditch, Hatfield, Stevenage and Basildon.

On 23 January 1947 Brett gave a two-hour presentation in the King's Hall to the people of Weston-super-Mare, in which he outlined a master plan that would create a garden city by the sea. This would involve the construction of a new railway station, a new coach park and an imposing new civic centre that would house an extension to the Town Hall, a health centre, a clinic, a youth centre and a large hotel. New tree-lined traffic routes would connect these with the main shopping centres and entertainment centre, and a 90,000-seat, multi-sports stadium would be created in the Town Quarry. Driving this new vision was the need to revive Weston-super-Mare, transform its damaged fabric and make the town ready for dealing with the proposed motorway heading southwards from Bristol, which would pass within a few miles of Weston. To cater for population growth, a series of eight- or ten-storey blocks of flats (18.3m or 24.4m high) would be built lining the seafront. Such monumental structures seem at odds with the headline underpinning the proposed development, namely that it should be a garden city by the sea.

The scheme required the demolition of around 120 houses and therefore the council served compulsory purchase orders on properties in the Carlton Street area. This was an area of dense, small-scale, working-class housing that was developing as early as 1841. To planners' eyes, these may have been regarded as slums, but this was a well-established community with a significant proportion of people who had lived there for decades. A public inquiry was held in 1957 and, during the following year, the Minister of Housing gave a temporary reprieve to 50 houses, but the demolition of others began.

However, Williams-Ellis and Brett's scheme of a decade earlier never became a reality – by 1959 it seemed a design from a different era, one suffused with post-war, new-town optimism, underpinned by dreams of endless government funding. The proposed motorway of 1947 had still not appeared, but Weston-super-Mare was nevertheless grappling with a significant increase in the number of cars, a challenge it initially met by using bomb sites as makeshift car parks. Therefore, in July 1959 Chamberlin, Powell & Bon (CPB) were invited to prepare a proposal for a new civic centre on a 5-acre (2ha) site between the Town Hall and the seafront.

The council asked for a scheme to include new offices, housing and a public library, with shops, car parks and wider streets. It also asked CPB to consider whether conference facilities, a theatre and swimming baths should be provided. Geoffrey Powell produced the firm's report in March 1960. It recommended retaining the Town Hall, the Albert Memorial Hall and Emmanuel Church, but between them and the sea it envisaged the creation of five 12-storey blocks of high-class maisonettes and a 22-storey hotel rather than family houses on such a central site. CPB's vision, illustrated in a model created in 1961 (Fig 84), included a library in the centre, combined with a swimming pool and facilities for large conferences, but the practice's research suggested the town had no need for another theatre. The conference hall and terraces would stand above a single-storey shopping arcade containing 22 units, with extensive car parking beneath. The scheme would have cost £3.1 million, but the money was not available and this vision of the future was never realised.

Figure 84
This model in Weston Museum, created in 1961, suggests how different the town might have been if the scheme put forward by Chamberlin, Powell & Bon had been realised.
[DP218758]

Reconstruction and development after 1945

While the grand schemes of 1947 and 1959–61 were never realised, wartime damage, Weston's growing population and the need to improve the town did lead to some concrete outcomes. After 1945 most government investment was necessarily aimed at the reconstruction of major industrial towns and cities, and the provision of new housing for displaced workers. A town such as Weston-super-Mare, and seaside resorts in general, were not usually considered priorities, but by the late 1950s, new buildings were beginning to spring up (Figs 85 and 86). Lance and Lance, the department store at the corner of the High Street and Waterloo Street, had been destroyed during the war and in the post-war years its site had been used as a car park. By 1962 it had been redeveloped, after a heated debate nicknamed the 'Battle of Waterloo Street'.[81]

In 1969 Weston also got a new theatre (Fig 87), not due to wartime damage, but as a result of a fire in 1964 that destroyed the old Playhouse, which had been created in 1946 by converting the former Market Hall. On the Boulevard in 1967, a new, modern telephone exchange was constructed in striking contrast to the adjacent Edwardian museum and library. These 1950s and 1960s developments, and other smaller additions in the High Street and South Parade,

Figure 85 (below, left)
Union Street was widened during the 1950s, when it became simply an extension of the High Street. The last surviving small houses on its eastern side were removed and new office buildings, shops and a Friends Meeting House were constructed.
[DP218536]

Figure 86 (below, right)
The ruined Boulevard Congregational Chapel (now the Boulevard United Reform Church), in Waterloo Street, was rebuilt and reopened in 1959. The adjacent church hall, another victim of the highly damaging air raid of 28–9 June 1942, was rebuilt in 1953.
[DP218516]

Figure 87
The new Playhouse, which opened in 1969, was
designed by W S Hattrell & Partners. Its brutalist
facade has boxed-out panels of textured glass fibre,
sculpted by William Mitchell.
[DP218395]

can now be seen to be of some quality and add something to the townscape. The same could not be said for the site earmarked for the ambitious Chamberlin, Powell & Bon scheme, which instead became Dolphin Square. The first shops of this unambitious, low-rise development, with car parking above, opened in 1965 but by the early 21st century it had become very run-down and was demolished.

World War II brought industry to Weston-super-Mare, including aircraft manufacturing; fortunately, many of the factories stayed in the town after the war and shifted to making peacetime products. For instance, the Bristol aircraft factory switched to manufacturing prefabricated housing and subsequently larger buildings, such as schools and hospitals. A helicopter production line was established in 1956 and in 1961 the site was taken over by the newly formed Westland Helicopters. At one time, it was Weston-super-Mare's largest employer, providing work for 1,500 people on its 88-acre (36ha) site. In January 2002 it was announced that Westland's Weston-super-Mare site would close, with the loss of the last 350 jobs.

In 1958 Weston-super-Mare Borough Council decided to actively promote the town as a base for light industry and offered to sell, or lease, sites or buildings along Winterstoke Road at Oldmixon. Council housing was also made available for workers wishing to move there. A large area of land between the main railway line and the loop line was initially filled with prefabricated housing and subsequently replaced by more permanent housing, including post-war Cornish units providing houses and flats. The Bournville Estate was developed around a large crescent and a central shopping parade, and now has a large community facility at its heart. The construction of the M5 motorway between 1968 and 1973 helped to stimulate the development of new areas of private housing at the east end of Weston-super-Mare, though it took until 1994 for a direct link road to be constructed. However, in contrast to all the good news for Weston's economy, 1961 saw the end of one traditional, local industry, when the Royal Pottery (*see* p 75) went into voluntary liquidation.

By the 1960s, most of Weston's tourists came by car, with fewer arriving by train than before the war. Steamers and their successors along, and across, the Severn were also in decline, due to the opening of the Severn Bridge in 1966 and the relaxation of licensing laws in south Wales. The last service landed at Birnbeck Pier in 1979, further undermining the pier's economic viability. In 1963 there was a brief experiment using a hovercraft ferry between Weston and

Penarth in south Wales, but it was never a success, despite the journey taking only 12 minutes and costing just £1.

By the 1970s, grandiose master plans must have seemed things from a distant past, and instead the decade witnessed only piecemeal development and rebuilding. The opening of Weston College in 1970 seems to have given the green light to developers to seek to build vertically, at the expense of the existing historic buildings of Weston (Fig 88). The spacious footprints of their gardens proved an ideal place to construct large blocks of flats; among the historic houses lost on the seafront were Etonhurst, Kingsholm and Glentworth Hall (formerly Glentworth House), while Villa Rosa, at the heart of the Shrubbery Estate, was also replaced by flats. It was against this backdrop that Weston's Civic Society was formed in 1973, its first battle being to campaign successfully to reduce the height of the proposed 14-storey Etonhurst flats to something more in keeping with the surroundings. One building saved in the mid-1970s was the former Gas

Figure 88
The eight-storey Weston College opened in 1970 on the site of the National School. Designed by Bernard Adams, the county architect, it was enlarged and updated in 1997–8 by Stride Treglown.
[DP218342]

Company Offices and Showrooms in Burlington Street, which became Weston Museum in 1975. The Civic Society would go on to open the Weston Heritage Centre in a converted coach house and warehouse in Wadham Street in 1986 and nearby the Blakehay Theatre was created in the former Baptist Church in Wadham Street. Heritage and culture were already being successfully mobilised to save some of Weston-super-Mare's buildings.

Piecemeal development and replacement continued during the 1980s (Fig 89). In 1980, the Albert Memorial Hall behind Emmanuel Church was demolished to allow the construction of a large extension to the Town Hall. The hospital on the Boulevard closed in 1986, following completion of the long-awaited new hospital at Uphill, and within a few years the site had been converted into housing. The site of the Victoria Hall, in the Summer and Winter Gardens off the Boulevard, had lain undeveloped since 1942, but it was redeveloped as flats in 1983–4.

Figure 89
Carlton Mansions, a large complex of flats on Beach Road, replaced the seafront bus station, which had in turn replaced early 19th-century houses.
[DP218310]

Weston-super-Mare suffered major storm damage in December 1981; the promenade was damaged, the Rozel Bandstand was wrecked beyond repair and homes at Uphill were flooded. This led to a significant programme of repair to the seafront, including rebuilding the top of the sea wall. Undamaged by the storm, the town's open-air pool continued to be used, but, despite being rebranded as the Tropicana in 1983, by the end of the century it was receiving an unsustainably large annual subsidy of £250,000 and closed in 2000.

Birnbeck Pier was seriously damaged by a fire in 1984; three years later, there was a fire on the pier head and in 1988 the Victorian arcade building was also gutted. By 1994 the pier was in such a dangerous condition that it had to close (Fig 90). In 1998 it was put up for auction and sold, but the new owners, White Horse Ferries, proved unable to make it a going concern. In 2006 the pier passed to the regeneration company Urban Splash, but the company's plans for the site were hit by the general economic downturn. In 2012 a firm of developers, CNM Estates (Birnbeck) Ltd, acquired the pier, but still no tangible developments have taken place. Weston's other pier, the Grand Pier, has been more successful as it was more centrally located. In 2008 it was sold to local businesspeople Kerry and Michelle Michael, but unfortunately on 28 July 2008 the Pavilion caught fire and was destroyed. The Michaels acted decisively and quickly and a new pavilion, housing a range of attractions and facilities, opened on 23 October 2010.

The major event in the town centre in the early 1990s was the opening of the Sovereign Shopping Centre, in 1992. Its construction necessitated the demolition of a multistorey car park, remnants of the Royal Arcade and the General Post Office. Nearby, a substantial extension to the Winter Gardens Pavilion opened in January 1992 and the new SeaQuarium opened on the seafront in June 1995 (Fig 91).

The creation of such a visible tourist attraction on the seafront could not disguise the fact that Weston-super-Mare, like other seaside resorts, was witnessing a significant decline in visitor numbers, leading to less investment in attractions and to the closure of many guest houses and hotels. By the early 21st century, seaside resorts were having to recognise a change in the shape and size of the tourism market and find ways to cope with the impact of climate change. In the next chapter, the story of how Weston is tackling these issues will be examined.

Figure 90
Birnbeck Pier, pictured here in 2009, suffered serious fire damage in the 1980s and closed in 1994.
[DP083541]

Figure 91
This photograph shows the SeaQuarium in the
foreground, with the Grand Pier in the middle
distance and the derelict Birnbeck Pier on the horizon.
At high tide, it could be said that Weston has three piers,
a claim only Blackpool can rival.
[DP218017]

5 Weston-super-Mare and the English seaside today

Challenges and a vision for the future

Until World War II, seaside resorts had a near monopoly of popular tourism, the shape of the railway network inevitably directing people towards well-connected destinations. However, as in the 19th century, growing wealth and changes in transport contributed to transforming the landscape of tourism; in the 19th century it was in favour of the seaside resort, but by the late 20th century, increased disposable income and improved communications were drawing people away from the British coast. By the 1960s, increasingly old-fashioned, cold, wet and even 'scruffy' British seaside resorts were being unfavourably, and often unfairly, compared and contrasted with the bright, new, warm and affordable, sun-kissed resorts of the Mediterranean. People who had been visiting Britain's seaside resorts for years, and even decades, wanted a change, and the Costas provided it.

As well as competition from abroad, there was competition from within Britain for people's disposable income. While a two-week holiday might be the centrepiece of a family's year, now often taken abroad, people also began to enjoy a plethora of mini breaks, long weekends, day trips and winter sports breaks, most of the last inevitably being taken abroad. Traditional seaside holidays were also increasingly being challenged by new types of attractions and the growth of leisure pursuits that did not require more than an overnight stay. Disposable income might take people with free time to theme parks, spa hotels, a meal at a fine-dining restaurant, a romantic break or a football match. People might also indulge in activities ranging from sailing to skydiving and Civil War re-enactments to car rallies. Simple pleasures like walking in the countryside and visiting Britain's rich natural and man-made heritage, once enjoyed by small numbers of tourists, had become mass activities by the early 21st century.

Britain's seaside resorts also suffered from a negative image. A greater incidence of homelessness has always been apparent at seaside resorts and this came under the spotlight in the late 20th century, as newspapers reported that former bed-and-breakfasts were becoming 'benefits hostels'. The seasonal nature of tourism at seaside resorts has had a visual and economic impact, with seaside towns in danger of looking drab and deserted in winter, and suffering from a dramatic drop in income. Notoriously low pay means that employees in the tourism industry do not have sufficient income to buy their own home, and

The Grand Pier after dark – at its end is the new pavilion, which opened in October 2010 after a major fire two years earlier. [DP218333]

125

therefore seaside resorts often have a plethora of rental properties that suffer from underinvestment. In contrast, many seaside resorts also have a large retired community, people lured by the sea, for health and nostalgia reasons (Fig 92). According to the 2011 Census, 20 per cent of Weston's population is aged 65 and over, compared with the national average of 16.5 per cent. The 2011 Census also found that 10.8 per cent of the town's population classified themselves as 'people whose day-to-day activities are limited a lot', while a further 11.8 per cent were 'people whose day-to-day activities are limited a

Figure 92
The abiding link between health and the seaside, once personified by bathhouses and swimming pools, is more often reflected today in large villas that have been converted into retirement and care homes. This photograph shows 17 Clarence Road North, a house by Hans Price, which is now part of a complex of retirement flats.
[DP218568]

little'.[82] Therefore, it is no surprise that around 10 per cent of Weston-super-Mare's population provided unpaid care for a family member. The presence of a large retired community inevitably adds to pressure on the finances and social services of seaside resorts, the conundrum of providing social care proving a growing challenge to all local authorities facing changing systems of funding and squeezed budgets.

Government statistics can be used to capture a picture of the economic issues facing seaside resorts. Indices of Multiple Deprivation, which examine a range of economic and social factors, are prepared every few years by the government. They reveal that seaside resorts feature frequently among the most deprived places in the country. In the 2015 Indices of Multiple Deprivation, of 326 local authorities in England, Blackpool ranks 4th, Hastings 20th, Great Yarmouth 25th and Thanet, which includes Margate as well as more prosperous resorts and residential areas, is 35th. North Somerset Council is a positively prosperous 224th by this measure, so apparently there should be few issues of concern at Weston-super-Mare. However, when the more detailed figures for the Lower-layer Super Output Areas (LSOA) are examined, the picture of deprivation in many seaside resorts, including Weston-super-Mare, is more striking. Of the 32,844 LSOAs, each consisting of approximately 1,500 residents in 650 households, local authorities with significant seaside resorts are prominent in the list of England's most deprived places. Five of Blackpool's LSOAs are in the top 10 most deprived in England and the town occupies 13 of the top 100 places, while Thanet DC and Great Yarmouth DC both have three in the 100 most deprived. North Somerset Council has eight LSOAs in the worst 10 per cent in the country, including almost all of the central area of Weston-super-Mare. Government mapping data shows much of the town shaded in purple or red, indicative of being in the worst 10 or 20 per cent.[83]

Economic issues are also reflected in the state of the fabric of seaside towns. Due to the seasonal nature of seaside tourism, substantial parts of a resort's infrastructure and many buildings lie unused, or underused, for much of the year and as they are generating no income, there is less incentive to invest in them. While it may be worthwhile to spend money on a garish fascia for a souvenir shop or an illuminated sign for a fish-and-chip shop, owners are more reluctant to invest in costly maintenance and repairs to the unproductive upper storeys of buildings.

As is the case with other seaside resorts, the changing size and shape of the tourism industry has left Weston-super-Mare with many large villas, and former hotels and guest houses, that have now been converted into care homes and, in some cases, drug rehabilitation hostels. Part of the town's housing stock has also become houses in multiple occupation (HMO), the presence of multiple doorbells indicating how drastically a building has been subdivided. The official government definition of an HMO is a property rented out by at least three people who are not from one 'household', but share facilities like a bathroom and kitchen.[84] These conversions are usually cheaply carried-out adaptations, with little concern for the impact on the building and its wider contribution to the townscape. Fortunately, most of Weston's seafront houses have been spared this fate, but the potential visual and social impact has prompted North Somerset Council to implement a planning policy in three areas of the town where no further subdivision can be permitted. The first area surrounds Moorland Road, the second includes Severn Road, Clifton Road, Clevedon Road and Albert Road, while the third stretches from Palmer Street to Ashcombe Road between Locking Road and Baker Street.

As discussed in chapter 4, underinvestment has been a recurring issue at seaside resorts since World War II, despite government initiatives to address some perceived localised shortcomings. Recent schemes have included the £45-million Sea Change initiative (2007–10), administered by the Commission for Architecture and the Built Environment (CABE), and the Coastal Communities' Fund, in operation since 2012. In 2001 the English Tourism Council recognised that British seaside resorts had 'the constraints of decaying infrastructure, designed for one era and not evolving, or not physically able to evolve, to accommodate the demands of another'.[85] A potentially vicious circle began to be evident at some resorts in which decreasing popularity led to less private income and public funding to invest in resorts. This in turn led to poorly maintained and underoccupied buildings, low-quality accommodation and unappealing entertainment facilities and therefore, inevitably, fewer visitors. This was amplified by negative media reports that gave the British seaside an unattractive image for anyone planning their well-earned family holiday.

At Weston, the plight of Birnbeck Pier and the surrounding area poses a major challenge for the town. When regeneration company Urban Splash took over the pier in 2006, there were grounds for optimism. A competition was held seeking ideas about the future of the pier, but unfortunately imaginative thinking was no match for the economic crisis about to engulf the world. The blight in this area has been compounded by the destruction by fire of the Royal Pier Hotel in 2010. Therefore, a once highly prestigious area, with grand houses looking across Prince Consort Gardens towards Wales, and busy with promenaders and passengers disembarking from mooring steamers, now feels separated from the rest of the town. While a solution to the future of this area is much needed, and often discussed, progress has unfortunately been negligible.

By the early 21st century, seaside resorts were also increasingly confronting issues arising from anthropogenic climate change. The fifth report of the Intergovernmental Panel on Climate Change (IPCC), published in 2013, provides clear evidence of climate change during the past century. Between 1880 and 2012 the world warmed by 0.85°C, though the rate of increase has been faster recently, averaging 0.12°C per decade between 1951 and 2012.[86] Evidence published by the United Kingdom Climate Impacts Programme demonstrates that sea level has risen around 1mm per year during the 20th century, but the rate has increased during the past two decades. Projections suggest that sea level will rise around Britain's coastline by between 0.12m and 0.76m between 1990 and 2095 if the medium emissions scenario occurs.[87]

As well as a rise in sea level, climate change is leading to increased storminess. Weston-super-Mare has known its fair share of extreme storm events, from 1607 through 1704, 1903 and 1981. Threats from large seas will be far from the mind of summer visitors enjoying its apparently sheltered location and the long, shallow, sandy beach left by the sea at low tide. Nevertheless, Weston-super-Mare has taken measures to cope with rising sea level and increased storminess. It also took the opportunity for a long-needed renewal of its seafront between 2007 and 2010, the first comprehensive project since the 1880s (Fig 93). This major engineering project was accompanied by new surfaces, lighting, seating and artworks. The project was supported by the Department for Environment, Food and Rural Affairs, the Environment Agency, the South West Regional Development Agency and CABE's Sea Change fund and cost around £30 million. This is a small price to pay to protect 4,500 seaside properties and businesses from significant tidal flooding, while upgrading the town's promenade and improving the appearance of the seafront.

Figure 93
The new flood and tidal defence scheme included the
creation of an additional splash wall on the road side
of the widened promenade and stepped sea defences to
protect the base of the sea wall.
[DP218045]

Figure 94
Knightstone Island's Georgian and Edwardian
buildings were underused or unused for many
years. However, they have recently been revived,
in part through conversion to flats. Modern blocks
of flats have also joined them on the island.
The barrage that forms Marine Lake can be seen
in the foreground of this photograph, with the lake
to the left. (See also Figs 66 and 71.)
[DP218360]

Enhancing the seafront may have been born out of necessity, but the quality of the finish has set a benchmark for other related projects in the town. The Princess Royal Square opened in July 2011 and provides a high-quality public space, with the listed, late 19th-century, cast-iron Coalbrookdale Fountain at its heart. The centre of town has been transformed by the creation of a new paved space in the Town Square, and Knightstone Island has had its public realm enhanced in recent years as part of the redevelopment of its historic pavilion and baths (Fig 94).

Weston-super-Mare – looking to the future

In February 2017 North Somerset Council adopted a supplementary planning document (SPD), a master plan and delivery strategy for the regeneration of the town centre of Weston-super-Mare.[88] The subtitle of this document is 'Living, Learning, Lifestyles', a recognition that the quality of life in Weston-super-Mare is of primary importance, and that a good place to live and work should also prove to be a good place to visit.

The SPD begins by outlining overarching principles; the first aim is to increase significantly the number of people living, working and making use of the services and cultural offer in the town centre. The second principle is to improve the quality of the town's offer and to change perceptions about the town centre, in an effort to kick-start regeneration. A priority will be the provision of at least 1,000 new homes, on brownfield sites stretching from the railway station to the seafront. These will be created in the area around the railway station, at the northern end of Walliscote Road on the site of the former police station and including the magistrates' court (Fig 95), and in the Dolphin Square area. Part of this last area has already been redeveloped to provide a cinema, an indoor climbing facility, a gymnasium and a range of bars and restaurants. As well as creating new housing around the railway station, which is also the location of the

Figure 95
The 1934 magistrates' court will be retained and adapted to provide new homes in the centre of Weston, but the 1970 police station behind will be demolished to make way for housing.
[DP218306]

Figure 96
This former Burton's store of about 1932, by the
company's architect Harry Wilson, has elephant
capitals, which are a common motif for a small group
of Burton's stores. It was not listed in 2017 due to the
loss of original detailing.
[DP218533]

main road into Weston-super-Mare, this area will be reimagined as a gateway to the town, providing a welcome to the joys that lie ahead for visitors.

The SPD also recognises the need to invest in improving existing housing, by limiting the creation of HMOs in some sensitive areas, and by promoting good practice. The desire to catch the tourist eye has led businesses often to compete rather than cooperate (Fig 96), and insensitive alterations by one householder can have a negative impact on a whole terrace or a street. In Weston-super-Mare, North Somerset Council is seeking to encourage property owners to work together to improve the appearance of their buildings and their street (Fig 97).

In a nod to the 1947 master plan advanced by Clough Williams-Ellis and Lionel Brett (*see* p 115), the SPD proposes that three wide, tree-lined boulevards should be developed along existing main routes: Station Road and Walliscote Grove Road, Alexandra Parade and the Boulevard. Like the 1947 proposal, the issue of their connectivity to the national road network is not clarified, as it lies outside the master planning area and beyond the immediate powers of the council.

Figure 97
The Centre opposite the Town Hall, a 1933 block of flats
above a shopping parade, has been renovated and
restored using consistent materials and colours, raising
the quality of the complex and the immediate
neighbourhood.
[DP218259]

The SPD breaks Weston-super-Mare down into nine areas –
neighbourhoods with distinct identities in which tailored policies and
development ideas will enhance the character of each area. These include the
commercial heart of the town in the High Street and Lower High Street areas, the
Station Gateway, and the Bay (the seafront from the town centre round towards,
but not reaching as far as, Birnbeck Pier). What the SPD carefully skirts around
are two key, and thus far intractable, problems: the future of the Tropicana
(*see* p 122) and Birnbeck Pier (*see* p 128), major relics of Weston's tourism
history. Although the Tropicana has proved adaptable for use as Banksy's
Dismaland in 2015, Icescape@The Tropicana between November 2017 and
January 2018 (Fig 98) and Funland during the summer of 2018, intermittent
use is no guarantee of a sound future, and a long-term solution is awaited.

The SPD still sees tourism as making a significant contribution to the town's
economy. The collection and evaluation of visitor numbers, and assessments of
their economic impact, are notoriously difficult and imprecise. However, various
figures collected and collated for North Somerset Council suggest that tourism
brings between £350 million and £500 million into the local economy and
provides between 4,900 and 6,700 full-time-equivalent jobs.[89] While Weston
may no longer be a destination for long summer holidays, a fact reflected in the
decline of the number of hotels and bed-and-breakfasts, it is still a popular day-
trip destination for people from Bristol, Bath and even as far as Birmingham.

Two of Britain's most prosperous seaside resorts, Brighton and Bournemouth, are enlivened and enriched by the presence of a large student body. In November 2015 Weston College was granted University Centre status, bringing Weston-super-Mare one step closer to becoming a university town. While it might never compete with longer-established rivals, this will add to the attraction and vitality of the town, particularly stimulating its nightlife and hopefully its cultural offer. The decreasing significance of tourism to the local economy, and the growth in the size and the status of Weston College, has led to the Winter Gardens becoming part of the college, providing new facilities for staff and students, while safeguarding the 1920s ballroom for use as a public venue. A building with an uncertain future now has a key role to play in the life of the town (Fig 99).

The growing contribution of Weston College to the local community and economy is seen as part of a shift from seasonal, low-paid and low-skill work to year-round, high-value, highly skilled, well-paid employment. The town is seeking to increase employment in businesses in the digital, creative, telecommunications, media and technology sectors, including through investing in a hub to support and inspire creative entrepreneurship. Seaside resorts once suffered from their relatively poor road and rail links to major population centres, but today the speed of a motorway is much less significant than the

Figure 98
This photograph of the Tropicana, the former open-air bathing pool, was taken in November 2017 while it was home to the largest covered ice rink in Britain, which allowed 500 people to skate at any one time.
[DP218337]

Figure 99
A large, modern extension to the Winter Gardens
opened in September 2017, providing additional
teaching and library facilities for Weston College's
staff and students. A cafe, restaurant and event space
on the site are open to the public.
[DP218509]

speed of an internet connection. Therefore, around the coast many seaside resorts are successfully welcoming 'creatives', particularly those attracted to a high-quality lifestyle in an attractive location. They are keen to stay in flats in the heart of towns, preferably in buildings with historic character. Attracting them, therefore, offers a way to regenerate areas of dense urban development that might in the past have seemed hard to improve.

The town centre of Weston-super-Mare is still dominated by small-scale businesses, where the ground floor contains the business but everything above is a potential financial burden. Historic England believes in the vital role that the accommodation above the shop plays in the townscape and could play in meeting housing shortages. Fully occupied buildings contribute to improving streets and neighbourhoods and generate the community atmosphere so vital to embed regeneration once the initial investment phase has passed. Alongside this is a desire to be greener, a philosophy encompassing everything from improved recycling and smart bins to enhancing the quality of life for pedestrians and cyclists. To this end, traffic between Alexandra Parade and the seafront along Regent Street has been largely restricted to public transport, and control of this key axis in the town has shifted to the pedestrian.

Public realm improvements in the town centre, on the seafront, in the Princess Royal Square and in the Italian Gardens have set a standard for Weston-super-Mare (Fig 100), but, as in many seaside resorts, there can be a marked disparity between the level of public and private investment and a consequent variation in the quality of the finish. While the SPD emphasises the need for high-quality development, recent experience suggests that private-sector investors can be reluctant to match the level of funding and the quality of finish provided by the public sector, as they are not convinced of the commercial merit. Continuing demonstration of the value and economic worth of high-quality new investment and sensitive reuse of historic assets is something that both Historic England and North Somerset Council see as a priority.

Weston-super-Mare as a town may be less than 200 years old, but it has a rich architectural heritage and a wealth of historic buildings. This architectural heritage will play a vital role in planning the town's future. Long gone is the belief that the future lies in wholesale redevelopment; the monumental blocks of flats envisaged in 1947 would by now have been recognised as a problem rather than a solution. Instead, the designation of the Heritage Action Zone in Weston-super-Mare indicates that the historic environment will be a vital part of the town's prosperity, an attractive town being a great place to live, work and visit. Weston's colourful past will make a vital contribution to its bright future.

Figure 100
The recently completed revamp of the Italian Gardens includes a collection of fountains to amuse children of all ages. This large public space at the heart of Weston is a place to sit, meet people and enjoy a coffee, and also links the town centre, the College and the seafront.
[DP218388]

Gazetteer

Birnbeck Pier. [DP218683]

1. Birnbeck Pier

Birnbeck Pier, designed by the renowned Victorian pier engineer Eugenius Birch, was constructed in 1864–7. Further additions were made in the late 19th and early 20th century, by which time the island was home to fairground rides. In decline since the late 1970s, by 1994 the pier was in such a dangerous condition that it had to close.

2. Worlebury Hill

The western end of Worlebury Hill is the site of an Iron Age hill fort with extensive earthworks and stone ramparts. The hill was used for grazing animals, Richard Parsley keeping a flock of 1,000 sheep there until it was planted with trees in the early 1820s. A reservoir was constructed on top of the hill in 1866 to supply the growing town's water needs.

3. The Chalet, 71 South Road

High up on the hillside and directly adjacent to the Town Quarry, The Chalet is an example of the fashionable 'Swiss' style, with deep gables, timber balconies and carved bargeboards. It is largely the result of an 1888 remodelling by Price & Wooler of a house of 1862. It was the home of the architect Walter Hernaman Wooler (1853–1936), who lived there from about 1885 until his death.

4. Town Quarry

The Town Quarry was established before 1815 and after the Enclosure Award it provided stone for roads as well as buildings. Despite its proximity to the fashionable houses of the hillside, and frequent complaints about the dangers of exploding charges, the quarry remained active until its closure in 1953. Today, the Weston Civic Society maintains a visitor centre and cafe there.

5. Atlantic Road

In 1859–61, Henry Lloyd designed Holy Trinity Church and the two impressive Atlantic Terraces on either side. By 1884 St Peter's Preparatory School for boys occupied the three easternmost houses of Atlantic Terrace East. The site had been taken over by St Faith's School for girls by 1914 and the inscription 'St Faith's School' can be seen on a carved plaque on the east elevation of the 1884 eastern extension.

Atlantic Road. [DP218554]

6. Anchor Head

Betty Muggleworth managed the sea bathing at Anchor Head during the early 19th century. She spread an old sail between rocks and under this primitive shelter ladies would dress and undress. At this date it was easier for people to get into the sea here than on the main section of the beach.

7. Claremont Crescent

Claremont House, built in 1816, was described in the town's 1822 guidebook as 'a beautifully situated lodging house' (Anon 1822). The house was demolished in the mid-1860s to make way for Claremont Crescent (1865–7), which has its convex side facing the sea.

Claremont Crescent. [DP218352]

8. Manilla Crescent

Henry Lloyd of Bristol created the two halves of Manilla Crescent in 1851, a large, gently curving Italianate crescent facing the sea. At its eastern end, Cairo Lodge, now demolished, was one of Weston's earliest lodging houses; it had been built as Devonshire Cottages in 1821. Behind the Crescent there was formerly an iron mission room.

9. Glentworth Bay/Marine Lake

Following unsuccessful schemes to enclose Glentworth Bay to allow bathers easy access to a body of seawater regardless of the tide, by 1929 a barrage had been constructed between Knightstone Island and the shoreline near the southern end of Claremont Crescent.

10. Knightstone Island

The first bathhouse and pool on Knightstone Island were constructed in 1820 and within a few years a causeway had been built to link the island to the mainland. The bathhouse, now converted to offices, was built in 1832. On 13 May 1902, the new swimming pool and pavilion/opera house opened.

11. Montpelier

In 1852, Henry Davies purchased 25 acres (10ha) of land to the north-east of the town centre for £2,100. Christ Church, the second new Anglican church in Weston, was built in 1854–5 to a design by the Bath practice of Manners & Gill. At the northern end of Montpelier, a reservoir was established in 1854. In 1863 the estate was described as 'the handsome and healthy locality of Montpelier, one of the modern beauties of Weston' (Beedle 1863). Hans Price designed a number of villas in Montpelier and lived himself in Tyn-y-Coed in Hill Road (now demolished).

12. Trewartha Park

Trewartha Park was named after a large house at the north-eastern corner of Montpelier. The street's southern half had been built by 1885, while the northern half was added during the 1890s. In 1898 Hans Price designed a group of semi-detached houses on the east side, including his own new house (now number 7), where he died in 1912. The west side of Trewartha Park was not built up until the interwar period.

13. Cemetery

In 1856 a dedicated cemetery opened, covering around 7.5 acres (3ha). It was designed by Charles E Davis of Bath, who had won a competition. It originally had two Gothic chapels, one for the Church of England and the other for Nonconformists. The cemetery was extended in 1917, at which date it incorporated the gate lodge of Ashcombe House.

14. Grand Atlantic Hotel

In 1859 the College, a private boys' school, moved into grand new premises in Beach Road. When the school moved out in 1889, the building was enlarged by John S Whittington of Manchester and reopened as the Grand Atlantic Hotel on 13 July 1889. The early structure is still recognisable in the centre of the hotel.

15. Open-Air Pool

In July 1937 the open-air bathing pool on the seafront officially opened. The entrance block was designed by the office of the borough engineer, Harold Brown, and is an essay in stripped-down civic classicism. The diving platform at the seaward end of the pool was very different, its elegant modernist form becoming a symbol of the town, frequently featuring in posters produced by railway companies. The diving platform was demolished in February 1982. Since the pool's closure in 2000, the site has been the venue for many activities, including hosting Banksy's Dismaland in 2015.

16. Corpus Christi Roman Catholic Church

This was the second purpose-built Roman Catholic church in Weston. The foundation stone was laid on 8 September 1928 and it opened on 6 June 1929. Designed by John Bevan of Bristol, it cost £16,000, a surprisingly large sum for an interwar church. The church is in the Byzantine style, with an impressive brick interior. It has fine stained-glass windows by the Harry Clarke Studios of Dublin and capitals carved by G Hillman of Weston.

17. Ellenborough Park and Crescent

Ellenborough Park is a large garden with villas to the north and south and Ellenborough Crescent, dating from 1855, at its eastern end. Henry Davies was the developer and W B Moffat of London designed both the crescent and the park. The name was a tribute to Edward Law (1790–1871), first Earl of Ellenborough, a politician and Governor-General of India, whose cousin was Archdeacon Henry Law, rector of Weston.

18. Sanatorium

The West of England Sanatorium for Convalescents was established in 1868. The foundation stone of the present building by Hans Price was laid in 1871, ushering in over a decade of construction. By 1875 the sanatorium had 72 beds and a Gothic chapel capable of seating 150 people. Almost £10,000 had been spent, but a further £4,000 was required to complete the building, which was planned to treat 100 patients (although by 1911 it had 156 beds). In 1890 a seawater bathhouse was constructed on the seafront. Today the building has been converted into private apartments.

Ellenborough Crescent. [DP218430]

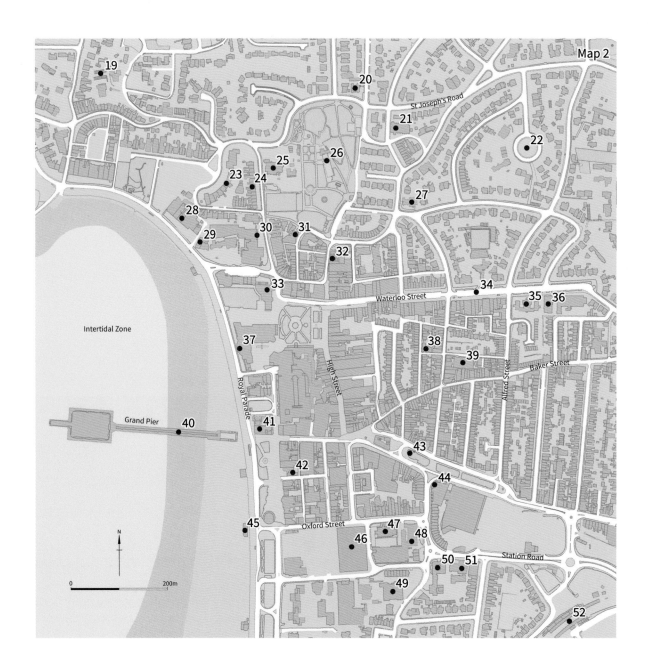

Map 2

Intertidal Zone

Grand Pier

Royal Parade

High Street

Waterloo Street

St Joseph's Road

Alfred Street

Baker Street

Oxford Street

Station Road

N

0   200m

19. Shrubbery Estate

Sophia Rooke (1787–1874) acquired this land during the 1830s and in 1844 she commissioned James Wilson of Bath to design the Villa Rosa, a grand Italianate mansion of pink limestone. Three other large villas were built during the 1840s and early 1850s. A second phase of development started in about 1859, when 30 pairs of semi-detached villas were planned and paths were replaced with roads. A castellated water tower, which overlooked the estate's communal gardens, supplied the estate. After Miss Rooke's death, a number of infill developments took place, including Shrubbery Terrace of about 1877. Villa Rosa was demolished in the 1960s and two blocks of flats now occupy its site.

20. 83–5 Upper Church Road

This pair of houses of *c* 1892 by Price & Wooler has a Moorish flavour due to employing horseshoe arches to the windows and extensive use of decorative tiles. It is said to have been inspired by a trip taken by either Hans Price or Walter Wooler to Spain or North Africa.

21. All Saints Church

The Anglican church of All Saints was designed by the eminent church architect George Frederick Bodley. Funding difficulties meant the church was built in stages, although Bodley's original design was largely adhered to after his death in 1907. The chancel was completed in 1899, followed by the nave and the north aisle in 1902. The north-west porch was added by C G Hare in 1911–12; the south aisle, chapel and undercroft were built in

Landemann Circus. [NMR 33489/007]

1925 by Bodley's pupil F C Eden; and in 1955 Robert Potter added a south porch.

22. Landemann Circus

Landemann Circus was part of the Grove Town development by the Smyth Pigott estate. It was named after Robert Landemann Jones (*c* 1816–1903), the agent of the estate. Large villas were built in generous grounds until the end of the 19th century. Several large houses, such as Lewisham House (now Eastern House), were used at some time as private schools.

23. Royal Crescent

Royal Crescent, like Oriel Terrace, was developed in 1847 by Henry Davies on a strip of glebe land he had acquired from Archdeacon Henry Law. Its name and form were clearly inspired by Bath, which supplied Weston-super-Mare with many of its visitors.

Royal Crescent. [DP218741]

24. Oriel Terrace

Like Royal Crescent, Oriel Terrace was developed in 1847 by Henry Davies. It was designed by James Wilson of Bath and is also faced in Bath stone. While these developments contained grand houses, they were soon providing lodgings for Weston's wealthier visitors.

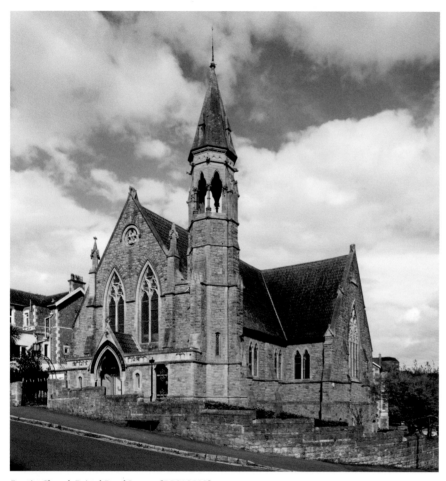

Baptist Chapel, Bristol Road Lower. [DP218508]

25. Parish Church of St John the Baptist

The medieval parish church was pulled down in 1824 and the new church opened the following year. The chancel was rebuilt and enlarged in 1837; in 1844 the north aisle was added and in 1853 a new porch was built. The church was repaired and improved in 1871–2 under the direction of Hans Price. The organ chamber was added in 1883 and three years later the vestry was enlarged. In about 1888 the porch was heightened and in 1890 Price & Wooler added the south aisle and new windows.

26. Grove Park

Grove Park was originally the private garden for Grove House, the home of the Pigott family, the lords of the manor. The land was released on a perpetual rent in 1889 and opened as a public park on 20 June 1891. A free library was established in the park in the family's former residence, but it moved to the new library and museum in the Boulevard a few years later. The park is the site of the town's war memorials.

27. Baptist Chapel, Bristol Road Lower

This fine Gothic chapel of 1865–6, by Hans Price, makes the most of its highly visible hill site. This was the second purpose-built Baptist chapel in Weston, after the Italianate chapel in Wadham Street.

28. Victoria Buildings

By 1838 the northernmost five of the seven houses that comprise Victoria Buildings had been constructed; the southern two, which are the least altered and are consequently listed, were probably built in 1840–1. By the mid-19th century a number of them were in use as lodging houses.

29. Leeves's Cottage

In about 1791, the Revd William Leeves, rector of Wrington and a composer, built a cottage overlooking the sea. When he died in 1828 the cottage was sold to a retired East India merchant, Mr Clements. It was later used as a dairy and today is The Old Thatched Cottage Restaurant.

30. School of Science and Art

A school of art had been founded in 1878 and the site acquired in 1885, but work on a permanent building, designed by Price & Wooler, was delayed due to funding problems. The first part was built in 1892–3 and opened on 14 January 1893. The school was completed in 1899–1900, when its fine elevation was added, featuring faience panels and carvings by J P Steele of Kingsdown, Bristol.

31. Blakehay Theatre

This was the first purpose-built Baptist chapel in Weston when it opened in August 1850, having cost just under £1,000. By 1862 it had become too small for its congregation and instead of an extension it was decided to let Hans Price remodel and enlarge the church. His work provided 400 additional seats and cost about £1,200. After closing as a church in 1985, it became the Blakehay Community and Arts Centre and is now the Blakehay Theatre.

32. Playhouse

The Playhouse is on the former site of Weston's market, which was founded in 1822. The first market house, constructed in 1827 by Richard Parsley, was effectively rebuilt in 1858 and again in 1897–9 by Hans Price. The old Playhouse was created in 1946 by converting the market hall, but a fire in 1964 destroyed it. The current building opened in 1969 and was designed by W S Hattrell & Partners.

33. Royal Hotel

Weston's first hotel was built between 1807 or 1808 and 1810 on the site of an old farmhouse that had apparently burnt down in 1805. The main body of the Royal Hotel dates from c 1810 and from 1849, when the northern section was built.

34. Waterloo Street and the Boulevard

Created in the 1860s, Waterloo Street, and its continuation the Boulevard, is a remarkably early use of the French name and this Parisian town-planning concept. Hans Price designed many buildings in these streets, including the Waterloo Gospel Hall (1876); the offices of the *Weston Mercury* (1885); the former Masonic Lodge of St Kew (1880–1; now the Constitutional Club); St John's Church Institute (1880–1); the former Victoria Hall (1882–4) in the first Summer and Winter Gardens, now the site of the Tivoli flats; a small Masonic hall behind it (1908); the former United Methodists Free Church (1875–6) at the

The Boulevard. [DP218520]

corner of Orchard Street; and the former Library (*see* 36). Price also designed his own office at 28 Waterloo Street.

35. The former Queen Alexandra Hospital

The hospital and dispensary was constructed in 1864–5 by Hans Price. It was enlarged in 1868 by the addition of the south wing and in 1870 new wards for fever cases were added. Further additions took place during the 1870s, 1880s and in the early 20th century. The new general hospital building, dedicated to Queen Alexandra, opened on 6 July 1928. The Weston Workhouse was built on the edge of the hospital site, behind a terrace of houses on Alfred Street.

36. Library and Museum

A Free Library and Museum was erected on the Boulevard as a belated celebration of Queen Victoria's Diamond Jubilee. The foundation stone was laid on 1 August 1899 and the new building was opened by Sir Edward Fry on 3 September 1900. The Renaissance-style building was designed by Hans Price in collaboration with Wilde & Fry and was extended in 1932.

37. Winter Gardens

In 1922 Weston Urban District Council bought Rogers's Field, the still undeveloped plot between the High Street and the seafront beside the Royal Hotel. Henry Butt offered in 1925 to meet the cost of acquiring the land and accompanying arbitration proceedings. The Italian Gardens were completed in August 1925, incorporating nine statues from Beddington House, Croydon, of which four remain. On 14 July 1927 the pavilion was officially opened, providing the town with a larger ballroom.

38. The former British School (now 1–6 Jasmine Court)

The British School, on the corner of Hopkins Street and Burlington Street, opened in 1855, making it the earliest surviving purpose-built school in Weston. Run by the British and Foreign School Society, it provided non-sectarian education for 150 children. On its opening, the building was described as 'handsome, lofty and well-ventilated'. It was extended in 1887 to accommodate 335 children and closed in 1918.

39. Weston Museum

The town's first gasworks was constructed in 1841 on land near the future Emmanuel Church. In 1856 a new, larger gasworks was created on Drove Road, about half a mile further inland. In 1912 the Gas Company completed a large block of offices and stores in Burlington Street. This long, two-storey, Classical building is now Weston's museum.

40. Grand Pier

After many years of discussions, work finally began on the Grand Pier on 7 November 1903 and the pavilion and its first stage opened on 11 June 1904. Designed by Peter Munroe, the pier was constructed by Mayoh & Haley of London. In January 1930 a fire destroyed the Pavilion and a new one was constructed in 1932–3, followed by a cafe and ballroom in 1935. On 28 July 2008 the Pavilion caught fire and was destroyed and a new building, containing a range of attractions and facilities, opened on 23 October 2010.

41. Site of the former Assembly Rooms

Weston's first assembly rooms were erected in 1826 by John Thorn and had a large room on the first floor for dances and other events. By 1840 the assembly rooms had been taken over by Joseph Whereat, a printer, publisher and engraver, who created a library on the ground floor. Later known as Huntley's restaurant, remarkably the early building survives in the block at the western end of Regent Street, facing the Grand Pier.

42. Former Commercial Cable Company office

The Commercial Cable Company constructed a purpose-built cable office in 1889–90 to retransmit signals, which were weak after having crossed the Atlantic via the company's undersea cables. The building, designed by Sydney J Wilde, was also linked directly to London by landlines. This three-bay-long building has decorative roundels depicting the company logo, which was the route of the cable across the Atlantic, and the initials of the Mackay Bennett Company. In 1962 the office closed and is now a bar/restaurant.

43. Alexandra Parade, site of the former railway station

Despite initial resistance, Weston became one of the first seaside resorts to enjoy a connection to the emerging national railway network when its station opened on 14 June 1841. In 1861 a separate goods station was constructed near the original station and there was also a room in Locking Road for excursion visitors. A new passenger station, with two platforms, a separate excursion platform and a refreshment hall, opened on 20 July 1866. During the 1880s the passenger station was converted into a goods station, which closed in the 1960s, as did the excursion platform.

44. Odeon Cinema

The Odeon Cinema opened on 25 May 1935, replacing the smaller Electric Premier Cinema on this prominent corner site. It had 1,174 seats in the stalls and 633 in the balcony. Designed by the Nottingham architect T Cecil Howitt (1889–1968), it was constructed by C Bryant & Son Ltd of

Birmingham and had a Compton organ with an illuminated console. In 1973 it was divided into three screens and by 2001 a fourth screen had been created.

45. Public Toilets

The provision of public toilets is a major commitment for seaside local authorities, who have to maintain facilities beyond the level that would be required for their resident population. Most seaside resorts have stand-alone toilet blocks on their seafront; at Weston-super-Mare, a block of public toilets of 1905 was built in an eclectic Edwardian style, with plasterwork and timber framing providing a hint of the Tudor style.

46. Dolphin Square

This was an area of working-class housing dating from the 19th century that was earmarked for redevelopment after World War II. An ambitious scheme by Chamberlin, Powell & Bon in 1959–61 was not realised and instead Dolphin Square was created. The first shops of this unambitious, low-rise development, with car parking above, opened in 1965. By the early 21st century, it had become very rundown and was demolished. In 2018 the site was in the process of being redeveloped.

47. Emmanuel Church

Emmanuel was Weston's first Anglican daughter church, founded due to the exertions of the rector, Archdeacon Henry Law. The site was donated by Richard Parsley and the foundation stone was laid on 9 March 1846 by Law, who had also contributed financially to the funding appeal, as had the Dowager Queen Adelaide. The completed church cost

£3,200, which was funded entirely out of donations; it was consecrated on 15 October 1847. The architects, Manners & Gill, employed a Perpendicular Gothic design with a large west tower.

48. Town Hall

A competition for a design for a town hall was held in 1856 and the new building, by James Wilson of Bath, was inaugurated on 3 March 1859. The original building was enlarged and remodelled in 1897, at a cost of about £5,000, by Hans Price to include new offices and a council chamber for the recently created Urban District Council. In 1909 a new committee room was added and the Town Hall was again extended to the north in 1927.

49. Board School, Walliscote Road

Comprising a main block for boys and girls and a detached infants' school, this was the first school to be built by the School Board, established in 1893, and it was clearly intended to be a statement, costing over £10,000. The school buildings in the Flemish Renaissance style are among Hans Price's best-known works and opened on 30 July 1897.

50. Magistrates' Court

A new combined magistrates' court and police station opened on 18 September 1934 and contained three courtrooms on the first floor. Behind the courthouse were four police houses, which were demolished in 1969 to make way for a separate, purpose-built police station at the rear of the 1934 building. Both the police station and magistrates' court were empty and unused in 2018.

Board School, Walliscote Road. [DP218986]

51. Victoria Methodist Church and Whitecross House

The current church in a simplified Gothic style was built in 1935–6 to a design by local architects Fry, Paterson & Jones. It replaced a church of 1899–1900 designed by W J Morley of Bradford, which burnt down in 1935. Behind the church is the former Whitecross House, the historic centre of Richard Parsley's Whitecross Estate and farmstead. It is shown on the 1838 tithe map and was described in 1840 as 'newly erected'.

52. Railway Station and Signal Box

The signal box beside Weston's current railway station dates from 1866 and is related to the town's previous station and branch line. It is said to be the oldest surviving signal box on the British rail system. The present station was designed in 1875–6 by Francis Fox, but there were significant delays and the station finally opened to passengers on 1 March 1884.

Notes

1 http://www.n-somerset.gov.uk/wp-content/uploads/2015/12/Weston-super-Mare-Town-Centre-Regeneration-Supplementary-Planning-Document.pdf [accessed 1 March 2018].

2 https://landuse.co.uk [accessed 3 April 2018].

3 http://www.alliesandmorrison.com [accessed 3 April 2018].

4 Anon 1913, 12.

5 Collinson 1791, iii, 611.

6 Baker 1928, no pagination.

7 Defoe 1704.

8 Anon 1847, 17.

9 *Gentleman's Magazine*, December 1805, 1099.

10 Baker 1928, no pagination.

11 Anon 1822, 9; Anon 1847, 13; Brown 1854, 9; Whereat 1855, 48.

12 Brown and Loosley 1979, 32.

13 Baker 1912, 4.

14 Anon 1822, 11.

15 Rutter 1840, 16.

16 Rutter 1829, 18.

17 *Bristol Mirror*, 22 May 1819, 2.

18 Ibid, 26 April 1817, 3.

19 Ibid, 8 May 1819, 2.

20 Ibid, 23 February 1811, 1.

21 Anon 1822, 6.

22 Baker 1928, no pagination.

23 Anon 1822, 19.

24 Rutter 1829, 27.

25 Ibid, 26.

26 *Bristol Mercury*, 9 January 1847, 4.

27 Anon 1822, 5. (Valetudinarians are people who are unduly worried about their health.)

28 Anon 1822, 6.

29 Rutter 1829, 22–3.

30 Ibid, 23.

31 Ibid, 23.

32 *Gentleman's Magazine*, December 1805, 1098.

33 Rutter 1829, 19.

34 Ibid, 20.

35 The National Archives, IR 30/30/452.

36 Rutter 1840.

37 Anon 1847, 51.

38 Brown 1854, 20.

39 *Weston-super-Mare Gazette*, 15 February 1845, 1.

40 *Bristol Times and Mirror*, 9 June 1849, 5.

41 Kelly 1861, 475.

42 Act of Parliament 5 & 6 Vict, cxx.

43 *Weston-super-Mare Gazette*, 13 October 1849, 4.

44 *Weston Mercury*, 17 January 1880, 8.

45 'Death of Mr Hans F. Price', *Weston Mercury,* November 1912 (transcript in file at North Somerset Studies Library).

46 *Weston Mercury*, 27 October 1900, 2.

47 Quoted in Jones nd, 30.

48 *Weston Mercury*, 7 February 1903, 8.

49 Beedle 1863, 21.

50 Brown 1854, 30.

51 http://www.allsaintswsm.org/church [accessed 29 March 2018].

52 *Weston-super-Mare Gazette*, 15 October 1845, 2.

53 *The Builder*, 9 September 1895, 99.

54 Beisly 2001, 57.

55 *Weston Mercury*, 29 July 1882, 1.

56 Anon 1847, 55.

57 Brown 1854, 18.

58 *Bristol Mirror*, 15 April 1826, 1.

59 Post Office 1866, 503.

60 Lambert 1998, 5.

61 Anon 1910, 35.

62 Hunt and Co 1850, 419.

63 Brown 1854, 13.

64 *Weston-super-Mare Gazette*, 9 April 1859, 4.

65 Morris and Co 1872, 451.

66 Anon 1847.

67 Anon 1910, 41.

68 Anon 1913, 11.

69 Brown 1854, 14.

70 https://archive.org/stream/kilvertsdairy020789mbp/ kilvertsdairy020789mbp_djvu.txt [accessed 13 April 2018].

71 Ibid.

72 Anon 1901, 10.

73 Anon 1910, 41, 45–6.

74 *Weston-super-Mare Gazette*, 13 July 1889, 3.

75 Anon 1924, 3.

76 Smith 2005, 134.

77 Borough of Weston-super-Mare Charter Souvenir 1937, 31.

78 *Western Gazette*, 26 August 1938, 8.

79 *Flight*, 9 September 1911, 787.

80 *Flight*, 20 August 1936, 201.

81 Poole 2002, 98.

82 https://www.n-somerset.gov.uk/wp-content/ uploads/2015/11/parish-census-profiles.pdf [accessed 23 February 2018].

83 https://www.gov.uk/government/statistics/english-indices-of-deprivation-2015 [accessed 21 February 2018].

84 https://www.gov.uk/house-in-multiple-occupation-licence [accessed 23 February 2018].

85 English Tourism Council 2001, 4.

86 http://www.ipcc.ch/report/ar5/wg1 [accessed 9 May 2018] – IPCC Climate Change 2013: The Physical Science Basis final report (policymaker summary), 3.

87 http://ukclimateprojections.metoffice.gov.uk/22530 [accessed 9 May 2018] – UK Climate Projections, Briefing report, December 2010, 8, 50.

88 http://www.n-somerset.gov.uk/wp-content/uploads/2015/12/ Weston-super-Mare-Town-Centre-Regeneration-Supplementary -Planning-Document.pdf [accessed 1 March 2018].

89 https://www.n-somerset.gov.uk/wp-content/uploads/2015/ 11/economic-impact-figures-2004-2014.pdf [accessed 1 March 2018]; https://www.n-somerset.gov.uk/wp-content/ uploads/2016/12/economic-impact-report-2015.pdf [accessed 1 March 2018].

References and further reading

Anon 1822 *A Guide to Weston-super-Mare, Somersetshire*. Bristol

Anon 1847 *The Visitor's Companion in Rambling about Weston*. Weston-super-Mare: J Whereat

Anon 1901 *Weston-super-Mare Illustrative and Descriptive: A Summer and Winter Resort*. Bristol: Cosmopolitan Advertising Company

Anon 1910 *The Official Guide to Weston-super-Mare*. Weston-super-Mare: F & E Phillput

Anon 1913 *A Pictorial and Descriptive Guide to Weston-super-Mare*. London: Ward, Lock & Co

Anon 1924 *The Borough Guide to Weston-super-Mare and its Neighbourhood*. Cheltenham: Ed J Burrow & Co

Baker, Ernest E 1887 *A Chronicle of Leading Events in the History of Weston-super-Mare*. Weston-super-Mare: Dare and Frampton

Baker, Ernest E 1911 *Weston-super-Mare: Village Jottings ... Compiled chiefly from interviews with the oldest inhabitants in the year 1883*. Weston-super-Mare: Frampton & Sons

Baker, Ernest E 1912 *A Few Notes on the History of Weston-super-Mare from 1326*. Weston-super-Mare: Frampton & Sons

Baker, Ernest E 1928 *The Village of Weston-super-Mare: Historical Notes*. Weston-super-Mare

Beedle, Thomas 1863 *Beedle's Popular Sixpenny Handbook of Weston-super-Mare and its Vicinity*. Weston-super-Mare: Thomas Beedle

Beisly, Philip 2001 *Weston-super-Mare Past*. Chichester: Phillimore

Borough of Weston-super-Mare Charter Souvenir 1937 *Official souvenir ... of the Charter of Incorporation*. Weston-super-Mare

Brodie, Allan and Winter, Gary 2007 *England's Seaside Resorts*. Swindon: English Heritage

Brown, Alexander 1854 *Brown's New Guide to Weston-super-Mare and the Neighbourhood*. Weston-super-Mare: Alexander Brown Family

Brown, Bryan J H and Loosley, John 1979 *The Book of Weston-super-Mare: The Story of the Town's Past*. Buckingham: Barracuda Books

Brown, Bryan J H and Loosley, John 1985 *Yesterday's Town: Weston-super-Mare*. Buckingham: Barracuda Books

Collinson, John 1791 *The History and Antiquities of the County of Somerset*. Bath: R Cruttwell [Printer], 3 Volumes

Defoe, Daniel 1704 *The Storm*. London: G Sawbridge

English Tourism Council 2001 *Sea Changes: Creating World-Class Resorts in England: A Strategy for Regenerating England's Resorts*. English Tourism Council

Foyle, Andrew and Pevsner, Nikolaus 2011 *Somerset: North and Bristol*. New Haven and London: Yale University Press

Hassan, John 2003 *The Seaside, Health and the Environment in England and Wales since 1800*. Aldershot: Ashgate

Hunt and Co 1850 *Directory and Topography of the City of Bristol*. London: E Hunt & Co

Jones, B C nd *Whitecross: A Study of a Weston-super-Mare Housing Expansion 1884–1914*. (unpublished typescript in Somerset Archives and Local Studies)

Kelly 1861 *Kelly's Post Office Directory of Somersetshire*. London: Kelly and Co

Lambert, David 1998 *Historic Public Parks: Weston-super-Mare*. Bristol: Avon Gardens Trust

Morris and Co 1872 *Morris and Co's Commercial Directory and Gazetteer of Somersetshire with Bristol*. Nottingham: Morris and Co

Poole, Sharon 1987 *The Royal Potteries of Weston-super-Mare.* Weston-super-Mare: Woodspring Museum

Poole, Sharon 1999 *Weston-super-Mare.* Stroud: Tempus Publishing

Poole, Sharon 2002 *History and Guide: Weston-super-Mare.* Stroud: Tempus Publishing

Post Office 1866 *Post Office Directory of Somerset.* London: Kelly & Co

Robbins 1887 *Robbins's Shilling Guide to Weston-super-Mare and the Neighbourhood.* Weston-super-Mare: Robbins

Rutter, John 1829 *The Westonian Guide.* Shaftesbury: J Rutter

Rutter, John 1840 *A New Guide to Weston-super-Mare.* Weston: J Whereat

Smith, Janet 2005 *Liquid Assets: The Lidos and Open Air Swimming Pools of Britain.* Swindon: English Heritage

Walton, John K 1983 *The English Seaside Resort: A Social History, 1750–1914.* Leicester: Leicester University Press

Whereat, Joseph 1850 *The Visitor's Companion in Rambling about Weston and its Neighbourhood.* Weston-super-Mare: J Whereat

Whereat, Joseph 1855 *Whereat's New Handbook to Weston-super-Mare and its Neighbourhood.* Weston-super-Mare: J Whereat

Wills, Anthony and Phillips, Tim 2014 *British Seaside Piers.* Swindon: English Heritage

Census information is collected from Ancestry (https://www.ancestry.co.uk) and the Genealogist (https://www.thegenealogist.co.uk).

Population figures are primarily drawn from Histpop (http://www.histpop.org/ohpr/servlet).

Newspaper articles have predominantly been consulted using the British Newspaper Archive (https://www.britishnewspaperarchive.co.uk).

For simplicity and consistency, the title *Weston-super-Mare Gazette* is used in notes, but this newspaper has been variously known as:

> 1845–56 *Weston-super-Mare Gazette, and General Advertiser*

> 1856–68 *Weston-super-Mare Gazette, and Clevedon Journal*

> 1868–1910 *Weston-super-Mare Gazette, Clevedon Journal and East Somerset Gazette*

Similarly, the *Weston Mercury* is used in notes but has been variously known as:

> 1843–55 *The Weston Mercury*

> 1855–69 *The Weston Mercury & Central Somerset Herald*

> 1869–1911 *The Weston Mercury & Somersetshire Herald*

Informed Conservation series

This popular Historic England series highlights the special character of some of our most important historic areas and the development pressures they are facing. There are over 30 titles in the series, some of which look at whole towns such as Bridport, Coventry and Margate or distinctive urban districts such as the Jewellery Quarter in Birmingham and Ancoats in Manchester, while others focus on particular building types in a particular place. A few are national in scope, focusing, for example, on English school buildings and garden cities in England.

The books are written in an engaging style and include high-quality colour photographs and specially commissioned graphics. The purpose of the titles in the series is to raise awareness in a non-specialist audience of the interest and importance of aspects of the built heritage of towns and cities undergoing rapid change or facing large-scale regeneration. A particular feature of each book is a final chapter that focuses on conservation issues, identifying good examples of the reuse of historic buildings and highlighting those assets or areas for which significant challenges remain.

As accessible distillations of more in-depth research, they also provide a useful resource for heritage professionals, tackling, as many of the books do, places and building types that have not previously been subjected to investigation from the historic environment perspective. As well as providing a lively and informed discussion of each subject, the books also act as advocacy documents for Historic England and its partners in promoting the historic environment through the management of change.

More information on each of the books in the series and on forthcoming titles, together with links to enable them to be ordered or downloaded, is available on the Historic England website: HistoricEngland.org.uk